Advance pra

BUYING
THE FARM

"For today's young, the economic future is far more bleak, and global warming an unprecedented threat. Out of necessity, many will be searching for meaningful forms of communal self-sufficiency, healthful food, and renewable energy. Tom Fels's captivating and profound reflection on one earlier commune, Montague Farm, founded in the 1960s, offers hard-learned reflections, some practical, some eternal, from a time when communes were the chosen path of many. Elegantly written. An informative and worthwhile read."

—TOM HAYDEN, author of *The Long Sixties*

"Born in conflict, Montague Farm continued through decades of tortuous discordance, but left its mark in books, films, and music directly derived from it. . . . The scholarship in *Buying the Farm* could not be more sound and up to date. Tom Fels is well known for his meticulous care with such research, and this book makes a significant contribution to the study of this counterculture and its people."

—RAY MUNGO, author of *Famous Long Ago: My Life and Hard Times with Liberation News Service*

"The Montague Farm brought together an extraordinary group of young people who created a community that promoted environmental activism, fused with a visionary cultural radicalism, and who struggled with the tensions between an ethos of mutuality and a commitment to individual freedom. Most eventually left the farm to move on to other phases of their lives, leading, ultimately, to a series of questions: What to do with the farm? Who had the right to make the decision? What values should govern the solution? Tom Fels tells this story with sensitivity and insight, and with a keen eye for the way in which high principle and genuine nobility were often intertwined with grandiosity and self-delusion. This book sheds light on the radical culture of the late sixties and seventies, and also on the painful process of its unraveling in subsequent decades."

—BARBARA EPSTEIN, author of *Political Protest and Cultural Revolution: Nonviolent Direct Action in the 1970s and 1980s*

"Tom Fels writes with eloquence, compassion, and ultimately wisdom about the mythical and magical place known as Montague Farm."

—GARY GOLDBERG, creator of *Family Ties* and author of *Sit, Ubu, Sit*

"Using his insider's knowledge Tom Fels has skillfully painted a fascinating picture of how a group of activists brought their own individual idealism and idiosyncrasies from the city to experiment with anti-materialism in the country. For nearly four decades they tried to make their own lives more meaningful while acting as good stewards of the land. . . . Although their 'back to the land' project succeeded on an individual basis, it failed to discover a new way in which a larger society could work together in harmony. Did our generation of the Sixties come to realize that communal living and the rights of the individual could not coexist for long? The land itself remained the living witness to their struggles and the dreams of their youth. Fels has captured that paradox perfectly."

—BILL MORGAN, author of *The Typewriter Is Holy: The Complete, Uncensored History of the Beat Generation*

"*Buying the Farm* reads like an ancient Greek tragedy, written in gripping prose by a master storyteller. The story of Montague Farm is filled with important lessons for those establishing new ways of living and organizing in the twenty-first century. Raking through the ashes of this 1960s commune, Fels does us an immense service by revealing the glowing coals, bitter embers, and enduring lessons of the final years of the last century, and the beginning of this one."

—ANTHONY SEEGER, Distinguished Professor of Ethnomusicology, Emeritus, UCLA

BUYING
THE FARM

BUYING
THE FARM

Peace and War on a Sixties Commune

Tom Fels

Foreword by Daniel Aaron

University of Massachusetts Press
Amherst and Boston

ISBN 978-1-55849-971-3 (paper); 970-6 (hardcover)

Designed by Sally Nichols
Set in Monotype Bell (OTF)
Printed and bound by Thomson-Shore, Inc.

Library of Congress Cataloging-in-Publication Data

Fels, Thomas Weston.
Buying the farm : peace and war on a sixties commune / Tom Fels.
p. cm.
Includes bibliographical references.
ISBN 978-1-55849-971-3 (pbk. : alk. paper) — ISBN 978-1-55849-970-6 (library
cloth : alk. paper) 1. Fels, Thomas Weston. 2. Communal living—Massachusetts—
History—20th century. 3. United States—Social conditions—1960–1980. I. Title.
HX655.M4F45 2012
307.77′70974422—dc23
2012030819

British Library Cataloguing in Publication data are available.

Facing page 1 and pages 186–187:
Meeting at farm reunion, 1993. Photo by Emmanuel Dunand,
courtesy Famous Long Ago Archive, Special Collections and University Archives,
University of Massachusetts Amherst Libraries (FLA).

For

Thomas Bezanson
Carl Oglesby
Arlene Bouras

℘

friends who shared
worlds of their own.

CONTENTS

ℰ

FOREWORD

℘

The Sixties in Perspective
A Personal View
DANIEL AARON

Montague Farm, the subject of Tom Fels's book, materialized in the late 1960s. It loosely cohered for the next thirty-five years "in different forms," as he puts it, until under intense internal pressure the community disintegrated in the clash between its personal and collective missions. Even so, it lasted longer than most of the earlier communitarian experiments that sprang up and collapsed in nineteenth-century America.

How did it survive as long as it did? Perhaps because it didn't stick to a rigid set of principles and was never stiffened by ideological correctness. It remained pretty much an ad hoc operation. The Montague "farmers" figured as adjuncts in a kind of "organic farming" and "recycling" movement—precursors of the current Green Party. Ideological issues mattered less to them than preserving the integrity of the planet. Other than that, I find no indication in Fels's measured account of a utopian vision. Rather, it's the story of a small number of self-styled mavericks who from time to time found Montague Farm a workable and even enjoyable accommodation—relatively undemanding, congenial, and cheap.

Montague Farm can be seen as a late episode in the long history of American communitarianism, but for me it has only a tenuous connection with the experiments in group living that sprang up even before the founding of the Republic. Nor can I liken the Montague commune to

Brook Farm's romantic enthusiasts or to the hard-headed members of Robert Owen's "Village of Cooperation" at New Harmony, Indiana, that flickered and faded between 1824 and 1828. By 1968 I had sensed a widening gulf between a loosely defined Old Left and the New Radicals of the time. The latter, I uncharitably decided, were too full of themselves and their personal grievances to work in tandem with the antediluvians of the over-thirty generation.

During my long engagement with writers and political thinkers who unabashedly challenged the assumptions of their respective "societies," I found what I was looking for myself in nineteenth-century American dissent and in the ideas and activities of our home-grown "reformers." Unlike the student activists of the 1960s, however, my allegiances were unharnessed and "extra-generational": they included young and old, male and female, wild and tame. Thoreau bulked large for me, as he did for the Sixties radicals, but more so Emerson, perhaps because he could cherish the cranks and eccentrics whose yawps once resounded in the antebellum United States—and keep his distance from them.

PREFACE

ℒ

Buying the Farm tells the timely story of Montague Farm, a commune
founded in 1968, one of the first of a wave of shared farms and alternative communities that swept the country, garnering national attention
and becoming hallmarks of the era. Montague proved exceptional in
that it survived in roughly its original form for the following thirty-five
years. The chapters that follow chronicle the role of several key characters—from the farm's founder, who lived only a year into its mortgage,
to the self-serving local organic farmers who for a lengthy period took
it over, to the farm's beleaguered trustees who eventually had to sell it.
Later, the focus shifts to the core group of farm family members most
involved in determining the long-range future of the farm. Charting the
interaction of these personalities, the story moves from the more familiar colorful trappings and passionate ideals of the 1960s into a present
in which the former farmers and their home face a new set of challenges.
These changes and the way the community reacts to them offer some
important lessons on the difficult task of living out our ideals.

What were the ideals of the 1960s? How did small independent
groups like Montague Farm help put them into action? What were the
forces that kept such groups together, or divided them? What was the
experience of such experimental enterprises for those who participated

in them? Did the ideals survive to influence the world around them? These are the sorts of questions posed by *Buying the Farm*.

Drawing on my own experience as a resident of Montague Farm, on decades of contact with the farm's extended family, and on the considerable writing about this period—from notes of farm-family members to memoirs, novels, and academic studies in the history of the time—I have tried to bring alive an era of contemporary history and to link it both to its consequences in the present and the future, and to its roots in the past.

It must be said that writing about a number of figures and a period of several decades has obvious pitfalls. The full story of the farm has been difficult to assemble and some of the individuals and specifics hard to pin down. This book is thus the closest I have been able to come to expressing my views of those people and those years; my interpretation is intended to hew as closely as possible to the events I observed.

Generally, in this book, public figures are fully named, while others, or those with lesser roles, may not be. The reason for the first is to preserve the story's genuine ties to history; for the second, to protect the privacy of those not seeking such prominent roles.

Regarding my own involvement, I came to Montague, as many did, more or less by chance. Attracted by rural life, I accepted the invitation of a friend to move to a farm for my final term of college. I ended up staying more than four years. By that time, and no longer by chance, the farm and its family had achieved a permanent place in my life. The book that follows is the story of that farm.

BUYING
THE FARM

What god was it then set them together
in bitter collision?
Iliad, Book 1

INTRODUCTION
Reunion Snapshot

Leafing through the photos of my former comrades, it all comes back. Here's Laurie setting up her teepee. She's traveled from the West Coast to join us. An occasional visitor to Montague Farm, she later bought a farm of her own and founded a commune some two hours away in western Vermont. Today she's an accomplished psychotherapist and the music director of her local symphony in Mill Valley, near San Francisco. There's Carl and Steve looking grizzled and tough out by the clothesline behind the house. In his youth Steve wrote the first book about Montague and went on to be an editor, writer, and social worker in New Orleans, Central America, and Southern California. Carl, at the time of the founding of the farm a struggling young author, is now a specialist in creative writing who teaches and writes regularly for periodicals and television, from pieds-à-terre first in Boston and New York, and now in Berkeley.

Here's a series of pictures of the big meetings we had in the barn. There's Susan making a point about the agenda we had developed for discussion. Her experience as a teacher and school administrator comes in handy now, as well as the tolerance she developed as a parent. In another shot, Irv corrects the group on a technicality, making use of his training as an attorney in Cambridge, New Jersey, and New York, a far cry from the rural mechanic and commercial farmer we knew a quarter century ago. Other pictures show Sam and Harvey, now well-known activists, following the discussion or contributing to it from their own particular points of view. In another photo, Anna, who worked with them on a series of political projects, holds a globe and speaks of matters of concern to the community as a whole. She now lives and works in Europe.

And there we all are sitting under a big tent out back, dinner having turned into informal discussion. Sam sits with Janice, though they no longer live together. Susan chats with her old friend Cathy, who now makes her home on the opposite side of the continent. In the background is the summer kitchen I once helped build; almost forgotten, it now serves largely for storage.

The year 1993 brought the twenty-fifth anniversary of the founding of Montague Farm. To honor the date, a large reunion had been planned. Celebration was part of our intention, but also work. At twenty-five, the farm was at a turning point. Issues we had ignored for years needed to be clarified and resolved. Music, swimming, and eating were to alternate with work groups and discussion, and a new generation, now the age we had been when we moved to the farm—Sequoya, Alpha, Eben, Nadja, and others, children of the early farmers—was to weigh in on the future of an institution they had simply taken for granted during the years when they were growing up.

The reunion drew farmers, former farmers, and friends from as far away as Germany, Africa, Seattle, and California, and from as close by as next door and the adjoining town. The goal was to reunite, to solidify, perhaps even formalize, the bonds we had long understood intuitively, and to forge a plan for moving into the future.

At the reunion, strong opinions were expressed about the importance of the farm. One former farmer described it as the hub of a wheel that held us all together, another recalled that it had served many of us as a portal from youth to adulthood, a home for a generation seeking community and personal growth. Others spoke of its role as a center for activism and social justice, a place where living took on a larger meaning.

Really, though, more was at stake than even our beloved farm. For many of our generation, such efforts at independence and social change had come to emblematize an entire era. Our work to reinvigorate our aging dream would reflect a wider public debate on the wisdom of our youthful goals and on our persistence in pursuing them. Was that era over, or could earlier ideals be adapted to move us ahead once again?

How well we succeeded at our work will become apparent. First, it will be helpful to glance at the larger album, to learn something about who we are and how we got here.

1
Origins (1968)

"Lazarus! More ink!"

It was the spring of 1968 and John, our venerable alternative-media veteran, was working at the press with Lazarus, a promising young recruit from Florida. A mailing deadline was looming and an important firsthand report by Steve Diamond, from the Columbia University revolt a few blocks away, needed to get out to the many underground papers served by the Liberation News Service.

"That's it. You're good," said John. "I think this is going to work."

1968: a legendary year. To those who lived through the era of the 1960s, it sometimes appears, in retrospect, as though almost everything memorable happened during that year. But 1968 had a larger context as well.

The scene for the era of the sixties was set in the warm glow of post–World War II America. Following the Great Depression and the Second World War, the young adults who became the parents of what would come to be called the Baby Boom generation reaped the rewards of their earlier efforts in a period of extraordinary comfort and relative social calm. Jobs were plentiful. Incomes were rising. Arts and culture expanded. Education and advancement came to be seen as integral parts of American life.

Looking back on this period, from roughly 1945 to 1960, an exuberance of living and design is apparent, as long-delayed needs and whims were met, that is still astonishing today. "Dream cars" and "dream houses" were designed to reflect Americans' highest aspirations. Americans traveled, participated in sports, and relaxed and retired in large numbers. Ambitious new buildings were constructed to accommodate expanded ranks of office and factory workers. New highways were built to facilitate transportation and trade. Novel technologies were harnessed to improve the lives of Americans: the jetliner appeared, the transistor radio and the television. New lines of consumer appliances and conveniences surfaced, largely unavailable before: the freezer, the blender, the air conditioner.

To recognize these as the comforts of John Kenneth Galbraith's "affluent society" is not to suggest that there were no problems. A war was fought in Korea, and the cold war with Russia of which it was one chapter was not resolved for nearly half a century. Unions struck for higher wages. Faith in our international leadership was shaken by Soviet advances in science. But overall Americans took these in stride. Such occasional lapses were not allowed to overshadow the prevailing national mood of victory and dominance. The educator Clark Kerr declared that with a cooperative young generation in development, the next few years would pose no serious challenges.

Other, discordant developments of the time, however, proved to be more accurate predictors of the era that would surface during the 1960s. In an age marked by affluence, discontent was growing visibly in the lives of children of the middle class. Among the most popular cultural movements in the country was the unruly new "Beat" outlook of Jack Kerouac, Allen Ginsberg, and their unsavory crew. Disruptive rock music began to be heard. Racial issues appeared more publicly, and the shadow of the atomic and hydrogen bombs pursued children into schools, where they dutifully hid under their desks in mock anticipation of a disaster whose sketchy imminence became a permanent fixture in their lives. The sort of students and citizens they would become would eventually prove a great shock to Professor Kerr.

Later historians and social critics see these as part of a larger pattern. What their parents viewed as occasional aberrations in their lives of comfort, the young of the late 1950s and early 1960s perceived as the less appealing aspects of truth peeking through. It was a matter of betrayal: looking about them with more educated eyes, the world as it was did not appear to match the one that had been described to them. As a result, they came to see the older generation and its province as compromised by complacency and a superficial sense of calm.

Cultural and political developments of the following era reflected these perceptions. The early 1960s brought the Civil Rights movement. From the mid-1950s on, the new excitement of rock music and the often politically rooted folk movement stirred the interest of the young in a way that big bands and Frank Sinatra did not. The death of their vibrant young president in 1963 ended for many any security they felt about pursuing motives for good in American public life. The funeral parade continued with the assassinations of Malcolm X, Martin Luther King, and Robert Kennedy, as well as the deaths of many less celebrated citizens working in the public interest. The mid-60s brought the birth control pill and the beginning of the movement to object to the Vietnam War. The late years of the decade saw widespread social unrest and continued youthful discontent, as drug use, political protest, and social change became the modus vivendi for youth across the country.

For the young people who started Montague Farm in the summer of 1968, the previous year looked something like this: Summer of 1967—the release of the Beatles' classic, paradigm-changing album *Sergeant Pepper*, and California's so-called Summer of Love, whose crash pads, venereal disease, and bad drugs often made it less blissful than the promised euphoria. Riots in the nation's cities—the subsequent *Kerner Report* studied 24 examples from a total of some 164 serious civil disorders from the first nine months of that year, calling them "unusual, irregular, complex, and unpredictable." Fall brought the immense "Mobilization" against the Vietnam War, at the Pentagon—and the initiation of the antiwar campaign of Senator Eugene McCarthy, who would eventually be credited with helping to force the sitting president, Lyndon Johnson, from office. Early 1968 was marred by the unsettling news of the Tet offensive, in which the North Vietnamese people demonstrated their will to win the war against us at all cost. The spring was marked by the deaths of

Kennedy and King. The Columbia revolt, in New York City, and intense protests in Poland and Paris, among many other places, brought campus resistance and political violence to new and very public heights.

Infighting and factionalism within the Left itself were also on the rise. Anarchistic political theater, such as that fostered by Abbie Hoffman and his organization, the Yippies, was garnering increased attention. (It was hard to ignore such illuminating gambits as brokers jumping eagerly for dollar bills dropped from the balcony of the New York Stock Exchange, or the dumping of industrial sludge onto the pristine carpets of the corporations that had produced it. Political demonstrations at the time were often visited by a uniformed young man with plastic airplanes on his shoulders who called himself General Waste More Land.) Significantly, the year would continue with the tumultuous Democratic convention in Chicago and the election of Republican Richard Nixon, a candidate the nation had rejected some ten years earlier, and about whom it had feelings that were, as it turned out, justifiably mixed.

In relation to this larger context, the founders of Montague Farm and their peers had been to some extent respondents to the world around them. To the scourge of war they had answered by developing a movement for peace. To assist their troubled fellow countrymen they had worked to eradicate poverty and racism; the sixties was the era of such socially and politically conscious groups as Students for a Democratic Society (SDS), the Student Nonviolent Coordinating Committee (SNCC), the Peace Corps, and Volunteers in Service to America (VISTA), as well as the War on Poverty and the Freedom Summer campaign. In response to the misguided materialistic excesses of their elders, many turned to a scraggly, severe personal look of old jeans and cast-off fatigues, topped by unkempt long hair and other signs of disrespect for authority and social order. In schools and colleges, questioning was far more popular, or at least more visible, than cooperation.

But by the time of the founding of the farm, its early planners had also become instigators of new approaches. In answer to the threat of violence, they were beginning to choose to live quietly on their own. Finding political activity increasingly polarized and self-serving, they struck out in new directions, emphasizing basic personal honesty and positive cultural change. To counteract the disenchanting spell of death, they chose activities fostering life. And taking urban political theater a step further, they fixed upon expressing through their own lives possibilities for new modes of living that could be demonstrated in no other way—in our case, something that came to be called the back-to-the-land movement. Such attitudes and actions would become emblems of their time.

Liberation News Service

Into this picture enter two enterprising members of the new generation. The founders of Liberation News Service (LNS) in 1967 were Raymond Mungo and Marshall Bloom. Both young journalists, activists, outstanding students, and editors of their college newspapers, they watched with interest the growth of a new national constellation of countercultural journals—the underground press—and recognized the need to supply them with political and cultural news untainted by the bias of government or the mainstream press. Joining forces, and taking the sort of leap now much associated with those times, they abandoned the conventional student press network of which they had been leaders, pooled their scant resources, and moved to Washington, DC, in the fall of 1967, operating LNS from there until mid-1968.

In his four years at Boston University, Raymond Mungo, the editor of its student-run paper, the *Boston University News,* had achieved, among radicals, the status of a minor deity. A political reformer from a working-class Massachusetts family, he had a humanistic bent, and he was at the forefront of a group that protested university regulations, state laws, and national policy. In this role, Mungo was often in the Boston papers or on television news. His championship of issues including birth control, labor rights, drug use, and the end of the Vietnam War made him a natural opponent to a number of institutions, including the one in which he was situated. To found LNS, he gave up a Harvard graduate fellowship and a promising establishment career, though he did creatively recycle the funds provided to forge his own bold new alternative path.

Marshall Bloom, scion of a comfortable middle-class family from Denver, had edited the *Amherst College Student* and promoted a number of political and cultural ventures at the college, including civil rights work, antiwar protest, liberalization of college rules, and a program to bring high-profile outside speakers to campus. High-strung but very effective, he was best known at the time for the demonstration he helped organize for his graduation in 1966, when members of his class protested the questionable choice by the college of a speaker for the occasion: Secretary of Defense Robert McNamara, the principal architect of the Vietnam War. In the year after his graduation, Bloom went on to organize political protests at the London School of Economics over the school's purported involvement in the policy of apartheid in South Africa. This earned him headlines in the British national press, but also the enmity of a number of Britons who were happy to see him return home at the end of the school's spring term.

Under Mungo and Bloom, Liberation News Service flourished for several months in Washington, where its coverage of the massive antiwar "siege" of the Pentagon reached an estimated one million readers. Following the fiery riots in the nation's capital associated with the assassination of Martin Luther King, and the muddy dysfunction of his Poor People's March, LNS then moved to New York City, where its reporting on the Columbia revolt in the spring of 1968 was conducted from offices only a few blocks away. These and other tales of LNS are told in Mungo's counterculture classic *Famous Long Ago* (1970), the first book to recount the prehistory of what would become Montague Farm.

To the youth of this fast-moving era, months looked more like years. At the time they occurred, the events surrounding LNS represented to their participants long periods of time. In the early summer of 1968, with the news service approaching the completion of its first year, its founders were already restive and searching for new fields to conquer and new causes to serve. They had also accumulated a group of colleagues and friends who conducted most of the day-to-day operations of the news service, to whom they felt ties of guidance and responsibility. Taking in the world of hardening political realities and increasing militancy around them, they decided, as Mungo later wrote, that infighting, violence, and intrigue had not been among their goals when they helped found what was then known as "the movement." In the spring of 1968, Raymond, his friend the poet Verandah Porche, and a few other close comrades, disillusioned by the direction the Left was taking, announced

Staff of Liberation News Service, New York, spring 1968 (detail). Photo by Peter Simon, courtesy FLA. Future Montague farmers visible here: second from left Cathy Rogers; third from left Marshall Bloom; to reader's right Harvey Wasserman (with drill); to his right (saluting) Steve Diamond; to his right (at rear) Steve Marsden.

that they were pulling up stakes and taking their own group of close friends to a farm in Vermont. Marshall soon followed suit.

First Faces

The group that arrived at Montague Farm with Marshall in August 1968 was thus largely drawn from the ranks of the radical Liberation News Service and its extended family in Washington and New York. It was the survivors of this group who formed the family I joined when I came to Montague several months later, in January 1969. Steve Diamond was a young journalism student and Beat-influenced writer at Columbia who had become the news service's main contact for its reporting on the recent revolt there. When LNS moved, he did too, dropping out of college to come along. He was accompanied by his girlfriend, Cathy Rogers, a self-described all-American "girl next door." Originally from Seattle and on leave from her marriage, Cathy had been employed by the university's press. Lazarus Quon, a teenage runaway from Florida, formerly known as James Tapley, who had renamed himself as part of his new life, and Alex Kelly, a middle-aged British ex-serviceman living out of his car, were adherents who had joined LNS in Washington in connection with the Poor People's March. John Wilton, a veteran of the underground press and the idiosyncratic communal life of the Lyman Family, publishers of the cult newspaper *Avatar*, was a fugitive from upper-class British life who had come to America to advance his profession as an engineer, only to find himself greatly attracted to the cultural life of Greenwich Village. John was several years older and far more sophisticated than most of us, but as he devoted the bulk of his efforts to leaving his past behind, he was in spirit as young as any at the farm. Tall, gangling Steve Marsden, originally from Iowa (to which he eventually returned), was a student at the innovative New College in Florida. Low-key and introspective, he had come to LNS through the peace movement, to which he was, and was to remain, strongly devoted.

About the time I arrived in early 1969, there were several other additions to the farm family. John Anderson and Susan Mareneck were an Amherst-Smith couple. Both from the Midwest—Minneapolis and Muncie—and each as spare as the dour Iowan couple in American Gothic, they were seeking the independence of off-campus life. John was a musician with a band, and he soon took up guitar-making as well. Susan was a painter working days in an area college library. Both adapted admirably to the rural milieu, and several months later they bought a house of their own down the road from us. Kitty, a minister's daughter, was a committed member of the peace movement who had heard of the farm through the underground grapevine. With her friend Pat, who arrived a little later, she pioneered the lesbian life that would within a few years become more widely accepted. Irv was an Amherst student from Long Island who had dropped out to travel and educate himself in ways not possible at the college. He and his friend Greg, a college acquaintance from rural Pennsylvania, returned from a trip to Central America shortly after I arrived and helped spearhead our first year of gardening and farming, in which they both had considerable expertise. Michael Curry was a college friend of Steve Marsden; originally from Arkansas, he was an intellectual with an affinity for building and design.

Then there was Marshall. He had been a colleague of mine in civil rights, antiwar demonstrations, and other political work at college. Knowing that I had taken a year off from school and was planning to return, he had visited me in Boston and recruited me for his new effort in Montague. Moving to a farm sounded a lot better than living in a dorm. I signed up.

In coming to the farm I was thus following a path in some ways similar to others there. Having only recently left behind the demonstrations and social experiments that were beginning to flourish on campuses at the time, in Boston I had tutored underprivileged students, and pursued a new life I had developed for myself in the city's decaying South End, writing, drawing, and playing music. It was appropriate, then, that I join up with what was, in the days of LNS, the more culturally aware faction of the organization, the one Raymond and Marshall had led to the country, back to the land, to pursue politics in a more cooperative and temperate manner than had been favored in the intense environment of twentieth-century urban life. While it didn't always prove to be, in fact, cooperative and temperate, this was, especially in the beginning, the way our life was viewed by those involved.

The founding of the farm, Marshall's role in it, and the farm's early days are treated at length in Steve Diamond's *What the Trees Said* (1971), the first book to focus directly on Montague Farm and its extended family. Of the stories told by Raymond and Steve, the one surrounding the move to the farm from New York is especially pertinent, as it sets the stage for the chaotic life that was to follow.

Precipitous, as was always his way, Marshall's steps to separate himself from the hard-line activists he perceived as aiming to take over LNS had been secretive, devious, and highly effective. In a tale much told and retold in farm circles, he first interested Steve Diamond in his plans to move from New York to the country. Steve, an urban type if ever there was one, and recently energized by his role in national journalism and the movement, was at first completely shocked. LNS had just managed to establish itself, and now its leader wanted to move it to a farm in western Massachusetts, far from the action it, and he, thrived on. Steve didn't understand.

But Marshall was a coolly calculating soul. What he had realized was that Steve, a writer who loved a good story, who in his coverage of Columbia for LNS had already demonstrated his inclination for adventure and change, would come to be captivated by the radical idea he had proposed, in which Steve himself would play a leading role.

Indeed this is what happened. After due consideration, Steve was soon on board with the plan, and before long, true to Marshall's canny estimation, had an idea of his own. LNS had arranged a benefit fundraiser. They had received permission to premiere the Beatles' new film, *Magical Mystery Tour*, in August in New York City. Why not use the proceeds, suggested Steve, to help establish LNS in its new home at the farm? In a series of quietly planned and executed steps, the founders of LNS and their collaborators arranged to leave New York the quiet Sunday morning of the benefit weekend. With them they took not only the box-office cash from the benefit, amounting to several thousand dollars, but also the press, collator, and most of the rest of the news service's assets and equipment. The move was complete. Come Monday morning, it was then the turn of their antagonists to feel the brunt of political change.

In retrospect, there were obvious problems with this scheme. (Significantly, "scheme" was the word we came to use for the many out-of-the-ordinary activities we developed to make money or accomplish other important matters of survival in our new alternative life. Such undertakings tended to be risky and of dubious legal merit. Their results were difficult to predict, and often they endangered others as much as ourselves.) In this case, the consequences of the move, known in farm-family history as "the heist," involved a counterattack from the injured parties left at the old office in New York, who soon appeared at the farm to claim physically what they saw ideologically as their shared possessions. The aftermath of the heist also included calling in the local police—the "pigs" hated by most in the movement. It extended to recriminations, lawsuits, and other unseemly behavior, leaving many in the radical and liberal communities very upset with the conduct of Marshall's branch of LNS.

Equally important to the story that would unfold, the manner in which the news service was moved from New York to Montague presaged the disorganized, unstable, self-absorbed life of the farm that was to come. In contrast to its laudable motive to move ahead and lead those around it, it managed in the process of reestablishing itself to fragment the support of its allies and to burn most of the bridges—including some that might be considered procedural or philosophical—that might have proved to be of future use. Who, after all, in 1968, could have been expected to support something that could easily be mistaken for scamming the Beatles? But emerging scarred yet unbowed, its idealism, exemplary of its time, still intact, the newly established farm moved ahead warily into the future.

2
Early Days (1968–1969)

As recounted by its early members, the first few months of the farm were indeed the time of "chaos" and "disorganization" described by Steve Diamond in his book. Looking back, these months seem a clear expression of the contradictions that had brought the farmers to their new home. With a mortgage to pay but little income to help pay it, with lighting from naked bulbs hanging from the ceiling, food from the local supermarket, and a television to supply entertainment and news, the farm in its early days did not differ significantly from the apartments and urban culture its inhabitants had left behind. As cars died from lack of oil and antifreeze and attempts were made to coax comfort from an outmoded coal furnace, as the Liberation News Service continued fitfully and Marshall shuttled between the farm and its various creditors, cleverly staving off financial ruin, the farm hovered on the edge between country and city, honesty and finesse, discovery and defeat, and the blessings and curses of the straight and alternative worlds.

The farm's material condition was paralleled by its social dynamics: principles were unclear, and action even less so. Who would wash the dishes? Who would work outside to help support us, and what was an adequate contribution to the welfare of the community? Discussions were held to determine who should be able to stay at the farm and who should be asked to leave. The youngest member of the farm at that point,

Linda, was a teenager. Should she have to go to school, as did others her age? Who was responsible if she didn't? As Steve Diamond wrote, in this atmosphere of disorganization "we had to suffer the fickleness of random energy." In layman's terms, no one really knew what was going on.

Beyond these difficult circumstances, another important ingredient was added to the mix. In such a new group of still-young people, in a time of evolving mores and styles of life, few were ready to settle down. As the months passed from August to late autumn, a number of the farmers came and went, and in some cases did not return. During the fall, Bill, Al, Linda, Marge, and Dave—minor characters here—all departed. Later, the lively and also self-named Wanka, who had taught much to the group about independent living, returned to her home in Connecticut. (In his book, Steve had admired Wanka for sleeping nestled in the hay of the barn and for proposing that each member of the commune have just one bowl and one spoon that they should each clean themselves.) As the coldest months approached, John and Lazarus, in search of adventure and comfort, decided to winter in a warmer spot. Now close friends who had bonded over the printing press and other LNS, farm, and personal matters, they chose Morocco. Earlier in the fall Steve Marsden had left to finish college, though he would eventually return, and one member of the farm family and an early partner in LNS, Harvey Wasserman (known to his friends, for his prowess at softball and alleged resemblance to the comic-book figure, as Sluggo), had stayed in New York that year to teach, returning to the farm only on occasional weekends. Besides the farmers themselves, urban friends often visited for shorter or longer periods as well, adding to the ongoing changing content of daily life at the farm.

Travel, expulsion, city ties: all of this, combined with the demands of the occasional serious visitor or newcomer, brought an unsettled quality to life at the farm. By the end of the fall, with numerous battles of citizenship, common welfare, and personal animosity behind them, the farmers had become even more wary and guarded. Fresh arrivals were looked upon with skepticism, and peers were evaluated with newly educated eyes. A January trip to Washington, DC, for the dispiriting Yippie-run "In-hog-uration" of Richard Nixon ended with Steve Diamond, Marshall, and others returning to a house literally frozen. Something would have to change.

This was the state of the farm when I arrived, just a day or two before Marshall and the others came back from Washington. The result was that our first winter was—as the writer Ambrose Bierce had so succinctly put it in describing the western pioneers—a battle to regain the meager comforts we had so eagerly renounced.

Take the question of heat. It was now our responsibility to keep ourselves warm. A clear-eyed look into the basement, however, revealed an ancient furnace cobbled together to supply hot air through a series of loose, uninsulated ducts. The fuel—coal—though still occasionally available, had been abandoned a generation ago by the sort of American homes most of us had come from. That winter we limped along, administering inadequate doses of coal that seemed to disappear regularly without supplying any heat, and later freshly cut wood that seemed to smoke much more than it burned, until we were forced to conjecture that there must be a better way.

Water came from natural sources on the property—a miracle, it seemed. But it appeared less miraculous when it was unavailable as pipes or pump froze in the heatless house. When all else failed we made regular trips to the deep, rock-lined well outside, hauling buckets up by hand. Light was, of course, supplied by the regional utility, if the bill was paid, though the old lamps we had scrounged or inherited didn't do a great job of delivering it even when it was available.

Keeping our cars running and in good repair was a new challenge, now that we were miles from town and without parents, service stations, or knowledgeable friends to help us. Many of our aging vehicles slept out the winter under a blanket of snow, or awoke to the adversity of the season only with considerable cajoling. What clothes and furniture we had wore down from the rough life we led. Any source to replace them was fair game, from family holiday gifts to the Salvation Army. When food ran dangerously low, we discovered that the government we had been fighting would help us out along with the other ranks of the poor. As winter progressed, this bottomed-out life occupied us more and more.

We had moved here and committed ourselves to making it work, but how was that to be done?

Soon, though, some of the challenges became avenues to change, necessity and insight alike leading to a new, invented life. Our search for heat led to a small fleet of far more practical wood parlor stoves. (We had learned this through use of our dependable kitchen woodstove, a gift from more experienced friends.) The efficient use of woodstoves led to a taste for drier wood; hence gathering, sawing, and splitting wood became a more constant and refined activity occupying a significant portion of our time. The need for a regular supply of water, as well as the best use of the heat we had attained, promoted closer inspection of the large house we occupied, encouraging us to better secure doors, windows, and various indescribable gaps against the wind and cold they allowed in. Electric light use descended to the essential minimum as kerosene lamps began to appear, purchased from secondhand and antique stores where they had languished unused for years. New friends with businesses such as logging, farming, and building salvage knew more about cars and trucks than we did and stopped by occasionally to help us out with our own. Dumps in affluent neighboring towns, we discovered, did a brisk business in recycled furniture and appliances; used car parts could be found inexpensively at local junkyards. Thrift shops yielded treasures far more interesting than anything found in the traditional clothing stores we could no longer afford.

As we assimilated these new pursuits, the patterns of winter stabilized into something resembling a way of life. Days were spent gathering wood, shoveling snow, preparing meals, repairing house and vehicles, or mending furniture and clothes, with perhaps a flourish of decorative needlework on the latter to draw it more firmly into our alternative world. We might sit around the kitchen chatting and waiting for the bread we had learned to bake to come out of the oven, or feeding one of our other small stoves to keep it warm enough to read nearby. Once the mail had come, we might choose to delve into some of the many underground papers that arrived via LNS with almost overwhelming frequency—*EVO* (the *East Village Other*), *The Great Speckled Bird*, *The Georgia Straight*, the *Berkeley Barb*—or listen to one of the new LPs we were sent for review. *Toe Fat?* Hmmm, never heard of that one.

Montague Farm, fall 1968. *Front row, left to right:* Steve Marsden, Marshall Bloom, Alex Kelly, Lazarus Quon, John Wilton. Photo by Peter Simon, courtesy FLA.

People talked to each other, learning more about who we really were. We meditated, thought, observed, and reflected. Cathy would do her bookbinding, Susan found time to paint. Writers would write, potters would pot, musicians would practice. This era long preceded the computer, so the Internet and electronic games were not an option. There was also, of course, smoking—both legal and not—as well as other forays into the mind-altering substances much explored at the time.

Off-site activities included visits to neighbors and friends, parties, work at the local co-op, and regular trips to town for shopping and the laundromat. Some had jobs: librarian, teacher, health-care worker. Steve Diamond, preferring work with few obligations that ended early in the day (and with a felicitous connection to journalism), delivered newspapers. Some chose assembly-line work. Occasionally, for recreation, a group would head out to Boston or New York.

Life as it developed at the farm that first winter achieved certain characteristic qualities. From concentration on solving our problems, on getting to know each other, on sharing the small world we inhabited, emerged a form of collective emotion. We knew ourselves better as a group, our foibles as well as our strengths. We began to think and act, to some extent, together. There was also an element of fantasy. Stoned stories led to an idealized view of ourselves that was at times entertaining, at others repetitive and less than insightful. Like others of our youthful generation, we were prone to adolescent thoughts and desires. Affairs and relationships came and went. Few were focused on careers or the long term in any form, excepting, perhaps, the life of the committed revolutionary. With books like *Trout Fishing in America*, *Cat's Cradle*, and *Siddhartha* in regular circulation, life tended to have a Brautigan-like quality—surreal, gauzy, indeterminate.

On the more tangible side, there was a high emotional content to much that we did. We reveled in the small scale of our life and work— fixing the carburetor, splitting the log, making the pie—in contrast to our earlier urban- or campus-based attempts to change the world in more comprehensive ways. We enjoyed our closer relation to nature, even if it often fought back, and made the most of the more recognizable flow of time that emerged from events determined by necessity rather than random choice. Noticeably, there was no lag time between idea and action. If you wanted a shelf, you built it; if you wanted to go to Chicago, you persuaded someone to give you a ride. Bouts of instant success tended to be followed, however, by periods of doubt. What was the next project or trip? Often it was difficult to tell.

Life went on following such patterns, both calming and limiting, throughout the winter. Fortunately, just as it began to seem that winter would never end, we realized that spring was in the offing. The very thought of it helped change the outlook of the new communal family forming at the farm. A quick look around us revealed neighbors. How did they live? Conversations with our peers at Mungo's Packer Corners Farm, to the north, and other friends, were also instructive; they were several months ahead of us in experience, sometimes more. There were other fortuitous resources: Cathy's mother was an avid gardener, and on the strength of her influence, seed catalogs were ordered. To support the future garden, a greenhouse was built. As we continued to learn from neighbors and friends, maple syrup and honey began to replace sugar in our diet and, in the early days of the co-op movement, sacks of rice and grain, and tamari stored in bamboo vats, began to supplant the paper bags of more conventional groceries we were still used to buying from the larger markets nearby.

Tentatively, the new farmers began to tinker with their environment. Marshall built himself a room in the barn. The living room wall was removed to give us a space more in keeping with our numbers. A tractor was acquired to facilitate our future in agriculture and gardening. These were signs of progress that we hoped would complete our transition from city to country, and perhaps with luck would set our course, and that of our generation, for years to come. It was a difficult winter, but we believed we would survive.

3
Farm Life (1969–1973)

Over the succeeding four years, the farm's survival turned to success—at least up to a certain level. As difficulties were addressed and our new environment unfolded around us, themes emerged that would become mainstays of our first few years on the land.

One of the first to make itself known was organic gardening. As we learned to appreciate raw honey, whole grains, granola, and fresh eggs, salads, and dairy products, it seemed a natural extension to plan a garden. Scanning the rural horizon for ways to make a living, it also occurred to Marshall that, like some of our farmer neighbors, he might grow a crop of cucumbers in our upper field to sell to the large pickle factory a few miles away.

In both cases, the first thought was simply to garden and farm in a conventional manner. One of our number, Irv, had market gardening experience and recommended commercial methods for both garden and farm. As Irv, our world traveler and mechanic, had provided us with the tractor and seemed determined to do a lot of agricultural work at the farm, we all nodded in agreement. From what little we knew, flawless crops and ease of production seemed an attractive goal. But soon another view surfaced. Through her mother, Cathy had become familiar with the organic method of gardening. This regimen, not widely known and still at the time considered a fringe doctrine, involved an approach

more in tune with nature: fewer chemicals, more recycling and compost-
ing, companion planting, working in harmony with the seasons and the
land. Cathy and a few others defended this passionately through a number of intense discussions and, with the help of a brief travel absence by
Irv, eventually won the day.

This decision established several important new directions for us.
First, it confirmed the nascent farm family's ability to work together.
By addressing directly the question of how to garden and coming to an
acceptable solution to a problem that had divided us, we had created a
model for future use. Though not everyone was happy with the decision, we did all agree to abide by it, and so moving forward we shared
an understanding of how we had worked through that particular issue.

Another important aspect of this decision was that it had been guided
by women. The impetus to move toward organic gardening had first come
from Cathy, but it was also firmly supported by Susan and other women
in the farm community, who made a strong case for it and helped explain
why it was a good choice and how it fit into a new life we could choose
to lead. This was significant because although at the time the women's
movement of this era was still in its early years, it was becoming clear
to the communards of Montague and its neighboring sister farms that
many of what would become the tenets of that movement—the value
of women's contributions, their potential as leaders, their independence,
and their equally valid vision—would prove in practice to be true. And,
indeed, as the farm developed over these first few years, women steadily
played strong roles and were often among the most influential members
of the group.

The basis of the decision to move toward organic gardening was a
vision of closeness to nature. Still only a few months out of the city and
our time salted with regular trips back, still tied to the movement and
in the waning months of a trying winter, most at the farm could not yet
envision the possible new life ahead. But those who supported the move
to organic gardening saw that it was part of a larger change we needed
to make. In this view, self-sufficiency and independence from the social
and economic system we were at odds with was largely attainable, but to
make it work, our focus would have to shift. As with the end of the Liberation News Service—which had ceased after its contested hand-run

press froze in its new home, a converted but unheated garage—some new thinking was needed to place ourselves in the novel world we had created. This thinking or envisioning led to a determination to detach ourselves more firmly from urban life and to live more simply, an extension of the lessons we had learned over the winter. Just as we would garden organically, we would live organically as well. This led to changes in our style of life that were, in a word, permanent.

The garden, though important, was only the beginning. The decision to embrace organic methods forced recognition of other needed changes. We would be depending on the land, hence land needed to be defended, protected, honored. This was not the stance of blind worship with which we had arrived. It tended more toward the concept of stewardship, that our relationship to the land was reciprocal: what came out of it would depend on how we treated it. This ecological, environmental view turned out to be a principle that applied to practically everything. In the end, it seemed to complete the circle many of us had made. Beginning in the peace and civil rights movements of the time, aimed at ending war and honoring the integrity of the individual, we had now expanded our view to embrace egalitarianism entirely in the need to be at peace with the earth itself. In the decades to come, this would prove to be the leading edge of one of the major concerns of our time.

The means to these ends turned out to be work. Again, living more naturally entailed an extension of what we had learned over our first few months: the need for more focused care. Our future garden and Marshall's cucumber patch had to be tilled and then planted. Once growing, the plants had to be tended—weeded, watered, pruned, pest controlled—all largely by hand. The crops had to be picked and, if not eaten, canned, frozen, dried, or otherwise stored. The cucumbers or other salable vegetables had to be transported to market; those that didn't sell had to be carted to the compost heap to begin the voyage again. The trade-off here was obvious. For our labor and care, we received a bounty of natural goods. We were also able to become less dependent on the "instant," mass-produced consumer products we disliked—those produced through the work and resources of others—and launch ourselves

Cathy and Michael discuss the new greenhouse. Photo by Laura Bradley, courtesy FLA.

on a satisfying but labor-intensive way of life whose lessons, we thought, would be apparent to all.

A further development of this kind occurred with issues of health. As we began to consider keeping ourselves as well as our vehicles and machines in good repair, as the palpable qualities of a more natural way of life began to be assessed, and with the eventual arrival of children, health emerged as one of the many faces of our newly recognized relation to nature. Encouraging good health in ourselves and others was, after all, no more than what we were doing for the land, the animals and chickens we were starting to acquire, or, in a sense, the buildings we lived in. As part of this evolution, all in the farms' extended family began to pay more attention to our well-being, both physical and spiritual. Yoga and Tai Chi became popular, and books on Eastern philosophy and healing began to appear on bedside tables throughout the farms.

As we moved ahead through our first spring into the following few years, these and a few other early themes became the foundations of life at the farm. In addition, over the longer history of the farm family they proved to be the areas in which our beliefs would come to be played out in the larger world. The garden and our involvement with wood and land evolved into a commitment to ecology and environmentalism. The pressure of men and women living together more intensely than they had as youths led to a broader view of women's issues and a much wider acceptance of their roles as leaders and full participants in all levels of life. Concern for health became the basis of careers in that field. Later the same could be said for education, political and social action, business, and law, all of which to some extent were recognized as areas of importance during our early years at the farm. Not surprisingly for a group of journalists and cultural radicals, writing and the arts constituted another strong vein. The list of articles, books, and films produced by the farm family is extensive. Other members went on to professional careers or serious personal avocations in the arts.

Although the farm was an independent enterprise attempting to chart its own course, such motifs fit well with other cultural developments of the time. For the post–World War II generation, such ideals as independence, authenticity, participatory democracy, self-expression, social concern, and defiance of authority loomed large. On all of these scales, the farm scored very high. It could thus be said with some justification that over its first few years the farm conquered the most essential of its initial challenges and achieved some of its most cherished goals. Such successes laid the groundwork for further progress in these areas and helped create a model for their later application in the larger world.

Not all of our experiments succeeded, of course. The cucumber crop did not fare well, probably due as much to weather as to inexperience, and Marshall's other foray into self-employment, a small candle-making operation, proved far ahead of its time. (A similar business in a nearby town is now a multimillion-dollar corporation.) For a short period we were touted as the new face of sustainable agriculture, featured in an issue of *Organic Gardening and Farming* magazine as, quaintly, "The New Peasantry." Our history in this area turned out to be uneven, with some eras and practitioners notably more successful than others, though an

offshoot of the farm in upstate New York, with the blessing of the magazine and under the management of Irv, did go on to pursue large-scale
organic agriculture successfully for a number of years. By and large,
however, the farm's inhabitants, old and new, embraced their life there
and over the years sought ways to make it work.

After the disappointment of Marshall's cucumber crop and Irv's departure for the farm in upstate New York, the mantle of the commune's principal farmer fell to Tony Mathews. A generous and warm-hearted trans-
plant from California who had come to the farm in its early days through
the peace movement, Tony soon took to building and gardening, two of
the farm's mainstay occupations. From his experience in the garden he
branched out to cultivating corn and other crops on a larger scale, selling
the bulk of them to local markets and the co-op we belonged to. Over a
period of time, he planted an orchard, helped guide the farm's large haying operation, and made other serious investments in the land and its use,
as well as renovating a portion of the house. Tony eventually stayed at the
farm for more than ten years, until he bought land and built a house for
himself in a nearby town, where he has raised a family and continues to
pursue farming and building. In their new town, as at the farm, he and
his wife are involved members of the community. They also continue to
maintain strong ties to the extended family of Montague Farm.

The Family Grows

Among other early faces, John Anderson and Susan Mareneck, on the
small farm they had bought down the road from us, continued to live the
alternative life they maintained for several years. The house, which they
had bought inexpensively at public auction, was restored in a creative
fashion in keeping with John's ability at woodworking and the spare,
unadorned style Susan had helped foster at Montague. They heated with
wood, and furniture and fixtures were often handmade. Canning, sewing,
and other home sciences were avidly pursued. John continued with his
music and instrument building, and musicians passed through the house
with some regularity either for practice with John or for one of Susan's
savory dinners. John was also one of several farm-family members who

at this time visited Cuba as part of the SDS-sponsored Venceremos Brigade. Eventually, he departed for medical school. In his spare time, he still builds instruments and plays in a band. Susan remained longer, with one of the musicians, moving after a few years to New York, where she raised her two children, made a career of teaching art to support them, and pursued painting and printmaking in a serious way on the side. She maintained the house for years as a vacation retreat, and both she and John remain close to many in the farm family. In early 2009 Susan returned to the area and the house full time to take a job with a local nonprofit social-service organization.

Anna Gyorgy, a recent Barnard graduate with an interest in politics and social change, arrived in the early years of the farm and immediately set to work, energetically engaging in farm activities of all kinds. Later her friend Peter Natti moved to the farm as well. Recovering from a serious automobile accident but undaunted by the wheelchair he had been consigned to, Peter set up a wood shop and became a professional cabinetmaker. Each spent many years at the farm.

Another early arrival was Sam Lovejoy. One of a group of younger undergraduates Marshall had befriended in his senior year at college, Sam had an independent, entrepreneurial streak. By the time he moved to the farm he had started a house-painting business employing several people, and he had other private ventures on the side. Sam had grown up in the area and knew something about farming and the nature of our local rural community. This was very helpful, although, as we were to find, these and most other matters he tended to approach in his own way.

Also a member of the long-term farm family was Harvey Wasserman—Sluggo to his friends. Harvey had become involved early on with the Liberation News Service in Washington and New York. A cosmopolite from the beginning, he commuted to these cities first from Michigan, where he was in college, and then from Chicago, where he attended graduate school. During the farm's first year, he elected to remain in New York to teach and moved to Montague only after the school year was over. He traveled often and was at one point in the late 1970s away for well over a year. Despite his travels, however, and even after later moving back to his original home in Ohio to help run his parents' business, Harvey viewed himself as part of the ongoing, permanent farm family. An inveterate writer, during his first year at Montague he completed work on a book about American history whose publishing advance helped provide some income for the farm.

Undoubtedly the largest single influx, and the biggest change in population since the farm's founding, occurred in the spring of 1970. A devastating fire at a nearby commune had persuaded its remaining members to pack up their VW bus and head for Canada, where they planned to resettle. This New Age family, which had lived in teepees and lean-tos, and sported the long hair, strangely styled clothing, and unconventional automobile paint job common to alternative life at the time, was not welcomed at the border by the authorities of our neighboring nation. Having already left their land and with few other choices, they headed back south to Montague Farm, where they knew they could camp briefly while they revised their plans and thought about their next move. Several years later—for some as many as thirty—they were still there.

This new group would have a complex effect on the farm. First, the farm would need to assimilate them. Indeed, surprisingly soon the new people has settled in and were quickly becoming part of the farm family: Chuck and Nina Light, a couple; Janice Frey, a single mother; and Smokey (Mark) Fuller and Judie Sloan, another young couple. Before long they even brought in some additional friends of their own. Next, some of the specifics of their lives would have to be addressed. Janice's child, Sequoya, only a few months old, whose father had died in the commune fire, was the first child to live at the farm. For a group of young people still investigating relationships and their own views on privacy and family, this was something new to get used to. Janice herself was still grieving. Nina and Chuck, owners of the VW bus—which proved very useful and was christened "the Chuckbus"—had complex histories of their own. Smokey, with a taste for woodsmanship, was soon to be seen walking back and forth on the road near the house shouting the traditional "Gee" and "Haw" as he set out to train a pair of young oxen, probably a pursuit that none of the original farm family would have undertaken on their own.

While the farm had dealt with occasional newcomers from the beginning, a group of this size necessarily brought change in its train. As the denizens of the Chuckbus acclimatized to the farm and the farm reacted to them, new relationships developed and shifted and some familiar questions again arose. Who was the farm family? Did new arrivals hold the same status as those who had come before? Where did sympathy end and genuine brother- or sisterhood begin? Such issues would occupy members of the farm through all stages of its life.

Eventually the immediate questions sorted themselves out through the simple ministrations of time. This subfamily stayed and merged with our own. As with everyone else at the farm, its various members attracted some and repelled others. They joined circles of friends or formed their own. Each had some sort of role in the future history of the farm and its extended family. Janice, especially, who stayed the longest, will reenter the story in later years. One thing was clear, though, to those who had experienced the farm in its earlier stages: whether one viewed it positively or negatively, life in the farm family had changed.

In the fall of 1969, one further defining event had occurred that strongly affected the farm and its family. After the closing of the Liberation News Service, after our first difficult winter, after the disappointment of the cucumber crop and the demise of the nascent candle business, after, as we learned, a failed attempt at a relationship, other personal issues, and increasingly serious messages from his draft board, Marshall made the rounds of some of his close friends and colleagues. He wrote a short will, drove the little British car to which he was so attached into an empty field, and ended his life.

The shock of Marshall's death, felt far beyond the borders of the farm, fell heavily on its new family. Why had Marshall done this? Why weren't we aware of the seriousness of his situation? How could he who had led us here have left us alone to figure out the farm's many problems and chart its uncertain future? The feat of a world-class dissident, Marshall's last act was his most radical. We would ponder it for years.

By the spring of 1973, then, when I left after four years there, the farm had achieved a certain level of success in its own terms. It was substantially self-sufficient, reasonably well tied to the local community, economically stable in a limited way, and well launched on a trajectory of living out—and, through its writers, publicizing—some of the important values of its time. These successes would form the base of future constructive, and we hoped influential, activities at the farm.

On the other hand, the accepted level of stability at the farm was low. In an environment geared toward subsistence living, few were making any sort of reasonable income by common standards. There was little money for the niceties of life. Our family, though growing used to one another, had never entirely accepted each other and, though functional in its day-to-day routines, still harbored schisms that prevented the sort of unity originally envisioned. Over time, this contrasted strongly with our three closest sister communities—Packer Corners Farm, in southern Vermont, its neighbor Tree Frog Farm, and our own neighbor the Wendell Farm—each of which was formed around a core of close friends and shared a set of continuing interests and concerns. In addition, Marshall's death had shown us that even in our ideal situation, where we had considerable control and no one else to blame for our problems, we could not always muster the social and personal resources to care for our own.

These were sobering thoughts, and as success of a material sort was not all that was sought at the farm, it is important to note that by 1973, some four years after its founding, most of its original settlers had moved on. Often this was to pursue individual paths not suited in one way or another to farm life, but in part it was due to the unsettling qualities of ongoing life at the farm itself. For while we had arrived at a workable sense of the farm as it was at that time, the relative success of having satisfied our original needs had led by then to a tone almost resembling somnolence. Detached from the larger movement, and without obvious challenges to be met, life at the farm, its future, and goals, were unclear.

For me, personally, the handwriting was also beginning to appear on the wall. Though replete with a small cadre of writers and a few others of a creative bent, the farm had maintained an overall ethos that was largely focused on effecting social and political change through living out an organic rural life. Physical work and what might be described as a New Age form of political correctness were the coin of this realm. To my eye, in the farm as it had then evolved, those focused on a broader cultural mission were second-class citizens, and this did not suit my own developing needs. Moreover, as Steve Diamond wrote in his book on the farm, the formation of couples, with their own personal needs and new joint life, tended to lead to their departure. I was now half of a couple, and this indeed was one of the results.

With most of those who had offered guidance or models gone, leadership and direction at the farm in the era following Marshall's death were sporadic and uncentered, a pattern that would reemerge at critical points in its history. And while the farmers were living out the life they believed in—something now called prefigurative politics—it was to outward appearances apolitical and a long way from the world of demonstrations and protest from which it had arisen. But this would soon change.

4

Renewed Activism (1974–1982)

Early on the morning of Washington's birthday, 1974, farm member Sam Lovejoy, after considerable study and soul-searching, performed the radical act that came to be known in farm mythology as "the tower."

In brief, plans were afoot for two nuclear plants to be built in the area. Only a few years out of college and activism against the Vietnam War, trained in political science, and conversant with Gandhi and Thoreau, Sam reached into his bag of farm and repair talents to test his beliefs. Taking aim at the weather tower erected to record winds at the proposed site, he loosened a few turnbuckles and sent the five-hundred-foot-high steel structure toppling to the ground. He hitched a ride to the local police station and turned himself in, single-handedly initiating a new era of activism at the farm and—as he had hoped—far beyond.

As he described it in an essay he wrote later for an anthology on the era of the 1960s:

> In 1973 I went to Seattle for a visit. I read in the Seattle papers about a massive leak of about one hundred thousand gallons of radioactive waste from a storage tank at a nuclear power plant at Hanford. . . . [S]ome investigative reporters found out about it. . . . [T]he AEC [Atomic Energy Commission] said the radioactive liquid wouldn't make it through to the Columbia River (which

would destroy the river) before the year 2700. Until then, the Commission assured us, everything would be fine.

That did it for me. I started reading everything I could get my hands on about atomic energy.

On his return from Seattle, Lovejoy was picked up at the airport by his close friend Dan Keller, a founder and mainstay of the Wendell Farm commune. "You will not believe what's happening in Montague," was all Dan said. As they neared the farm, they rounded a corner that gave a view out into the countryside. In the darkness, the tower appeared over the nearby farms and woods. It seemed to loom enormously high and was blinking with strobe lights. "What the fuck is that?" Lovejoy asked in his characteristic personal patois. Told what it was, he mused, "A twin nuclear power plant on the Montague Plains, not more than three miles from the farm? It blew my mind. . . . 'Someone's gotta knock that thing down' were the first words out of my mouth."

From this single act emerged a chain of events that was surprisingly long and that largely defined the next era in the history of the farm. Along with Sam's act went the statement he had written to explain it. From the act and the statement evolved his trial for "malicious destruction of personal property" (the tower), a felony offense. Connected with the trial was a grassroots effort at local organizing coordinated by Sam and others in his circle. From the trial and the push to organize came a film on Sam and the dangers that motivated him. The film and the growing notoriety of Sam and the antinuclear cause were then leveraged for use at a wider level of organizing, first regional, then national. Before this cycle was over and Sam had returned to his grass roots in Montague, some six years had gone by and his life and that of the farm had been substantially changed.

Much has been written about Sam's story, and it need not be recounted in detail here. But to tie it into the farm's history and explain its significance to later events there, a summary of this period is essential.

Sam's statement in connection with the tower was widely published and discussed. In it, using classic traditional American formulations of democracy, the rights of individuals and communities, and the sanctity of health and well-being, along with an assortment of well-placed arguments highlighting his concern for the area and its citizens, he made the case that he had acted out of necessity and according to his conscience to remedy the intrusion of corporate and government power into community life.

By committing a crime, albeit a nonviolent one aimed only at civil disobedience, he had entitled himself to a trial. Through the trial, he intended to dramatize his concerns and bring them to the attention of the public, whom he hoped, when informed, would realize the need to take action themselves. It was a well-thought-out strategy—risky, though perhaps less so when weighed against the dangers as he saw them.

The trial itself, in the late summer and early fall of 1974, widely watched and reported, constituted a carefully orchestrated presentation of Sam's views. Expert witnesses were called, including such prominent figures as the nuclear expert John Gofman and the historian Howard Zinn, who could speak with authority on the issues he wished to highlight. The jury was courted through ample reference to community ties and concerns. Sam himself testified, demonstrating that he had no fear of democracy or the law if fairly applied.

In the end, though later informal inquiries suggested that he might have been found not guilty on the merits of the case—that his act was not malicious—Sam was instead acquitted on a technicality. The indictment had specified the destruction of personal property, but tax records clearly showed that the tower was real property owned by a utility company. Sam went free.

Sam lost the total victory he would have liked, the blessing of a jury, but in the education and publicity connected with the trial, he had gained substantial ground for his cause. This was on a par with other movement actions, such as demonstrations, strikes, broadsides, and speeches, that make up part of a larger political strategy. In this sense, Sam's story up to this point is very much in the tradition of the farm and its history, and so can be seen as an extension of it. Because of the break in time and the novelty of the cause, however, it would seem in retrospect to represent less of a direct continuation and more the opening of an entire new era. At this point, what can be said with certainty is that Sam had reawakened the combative political spirit of the farm. Although, as will become apparent, he went on to further expand his activist achievements, it would not be dismissive but complimentary to say that this was Sam's finest moment.

Realizing the importance of these developments, members of the farm's extended family set out to make a film based on the trial and its surrounding milieu. *Lovejoy's Nuclear War*, completed by Dan Keller and Chuck Light's newly founded Green Mountain Post film company in 1975, used the events of the previous year to create a more portable public statement of the goals of Sam and the growing antinuclear movement. Though ostensibly framed with evenhanded rationality, *Lovejoy's Nuclear War* was planned as an educational and organizing tool meant to carry the message that it was time to unite to work against nuclear power. In the coming months and years, it was widely used for that purpose. Often farm-family members active along with Sam in the antinuclear movement—especially Anna Gyorgy and Harvey Wasserman—would tour to show the film and speak. One effect of their travel and work was the quick dissemination of their message and considerable success at further organizing, from the local to the national level. A second result turned out to be that some farm members were again players on a much larger stage. Sam in particular evolved into something of an alternative national folk hero, which seemed to suit him, but Harvey and Anna were not far behind. Each developed a following and a role in this new movement that, as with Sam, propelled them to further accomplishments. All of these activities moved through the farm and affected it in serious ways.

Even before the trial and the film, organizing had begun for a grassroots antinuclear movement based in Montague. Beginning to spread their message locally, members of the farm first helped start an organization called NOPE (Nuclear Objectors for a Pure Environment). This group focused on education and on electoral and ballot measures. Through the NO (Nuclear Objectors) party, Anna Gyorgy was put forward as a candidate for select person, and Sam Lovejoy for town-meeting member. A referendum on the proposed Montague nuclear power plants was also successfully placed on the local ballot.

Moving to a broader local level, in the summer of 1974 farm members helped organize the Franklin County Alternative Energy Coalition, which with typical counterculture humor they enjoyed calling "the AEC" for short, twitting the national agency they opposed, the Atomic Energy Commission, which shared the same acronym. The Alternative Energy Coalition pursued education and a widespread set of programs, eventually including the canvassing of voters in all of the county's twenty-six towns and an antinuclear referendum covering the much larger state senatorial district it was in. With its Toward Tomorrow Fair in 1975, the group introduced a key element of its vision, alternative energy: solutions that might be pursued to avoid the need for atomic and other planet-unfriendly forms of power. On the home front, they began incorporating some of these changes into the farm. In part for themselves, in part as an example to others, they better insulated the house, installed solar collectors, expanded the greenhouse, and refined their agricultural tools to include solar food dryers.

The sequence of tower, trial, film, and organizing was accompanied by a great deal of writing. Steve Diamond, Harvey Wasserman, and activist Marty Jezer of Packer Corners Farm all wrote nationally about Sam and the new movement against nuclear power. Films were written and produced, and Anna and Harvey published books on it. Two points about this are relevant here. One is the tone. Although certainly the antinuclear cause was large and important, Harvey in particular tended to express the debate in terms of the desperate and colossal. Words like "catastrophic," "absurd," and "epic" dot his numerous writings on this subject, a trait that will later reappear. Sam, though perhaps a bit more adept, often took a similar tack. The other point of interest is the paradigm that the farmers-turned-reformers seemed always comfortable addressing suggestions to others. As would later be noted, the farm-based leaders of the antinuclear movement were charismatic personalities and capable individuals. While this stood them in good stead in the early days of the movement and the farm, it would later—as in some other similarly altruistic enterprises of their generation—lead to conflicts they could not foresee.

The Clamshell Alliance

In the next chapter of their tale, the Montague farmers moved up to a regional level of organizing. In July 1976, commencement of construction on another set of twin nuclear power plants, this time in Seabrook, New Hampshire, some two hours away, alerted the activists of Montague to the need to apply their talents farther afield. Shortly after the announcement of construction, farm members were in New Hampshire to help form the Clamshell Alliance, a new group founded to stop the construction of the plants at Seabrook, as well as any others planned throughout New England. (The organization was named for the sea life that would be endangered by the plants' operation.) Its founding statement emphasized the education of citizens and their right to control the lives of their communities. Its actions were to be nonviolent. Its positive invocations included man's ties to the environment, meeting energy needs through alternative sources, and freeing both nature and consumers from exploitation for private profit.

As a regional umbrella organization envisioned to coordinate the activities of a number of local groups, Clamshell had high ambitions and was inevitably a much larger and more complex organization than the local ones the farmers had previously been involved in. Inspired by the successful recent effort of European activists to stop a nuclear power plant in Germany through a yearlong occupation by some 27,000 people, Clamshell, or "the Clam," as they came to call themselves, chose occupation of the Seabrook site as their principal strategy. To coordinate its many groups, it adopted a decentralized structure that emphasized autonomy at the local level. Each small group was represented on the Clam's central committee; decisions were to be made by consensus only. While occasionally unwieldy, this leaderless form of organization, very popular at the time with activists and theorists alike, ensured that all members were involved all the time. Occupations were built around affinity groups, mini-communities that preserved in action the democratic structure set out in the Clam's larger principles and organization.

With this clear, deliberately democratic structure in place, Clam organizers went on to a series of actions over the next two years that moved steadily toward achieving their goals and gained a great deal of publicity

Readying posters for Seabrook, 1976. Photo by Lionel Delevingne, courtesy FLA.

for their cause. On August 8, 1976, less than a month after the formation of Clamshell, eighteen determined nuclear objectors walked onto the Seabrook site backed by a support demonstration of some six hundred others nearby. On August 21, 180 demonstrators occupied the site. In October, Clamshell held an alternative energy fair. At the end of the following April, after much planning and training, a nonviolent force of some 2,400 protesters attempted to occupy the site. An unprecedented 1,400 of them were arrested. Their boisterous two-week incarceration in New Hampshire state armories created a combination of strong bonding, self-education, and lessons in management. It also provided an inviting target for extensive coverage by the national media.

So far, the Clam had done very well. In less than a year, it had substantially raised the visibility of its cause. It had gained plaudits for acting on its principles. It had successfully challenged corporate and governmental agendas. It had created an organization that seemed to function well, despite its size, geographic diversity, and cumbersome internal procedures. It was the last of these that eventually led to problems that affected the organization, while at the same time reflecting its ties to the farm.

The farm members who played important roles in the Clamshell Alliance always stressed the local, democratic character of the antinuclear movement: that the strength of its larger organizations emanated from the smaller community groups on which they were based. The alliance's self-sufficient, small-town farmer mentors allowed it to claim a literally grassroots status. But the democratic model of organization also made it difficult at times for those who had originally envisioned it to encourage the group to move in the direction they believed it should go. Over the year of planning that was to lay out the next action, a large occupation slated for Seabrook in late June 1978, a complex dispute arose over the best strategy to achieve the goal of derailing nuclear power in the Northeast. In brief, a faction had developed—largely composed of new, more militant members based in Boston—that believed that activists should directly block the building of the plant. The farm-based founders of the organization and their allies wanted instead to hold to the principle of nonviolence and conduct a less confrontational, more nuanced, community-based long-range strategy. The argument that ensued focused on the fence that had recently been erected around the site. Should it be torn down (violent) or in some productive way respected (nonviolent)? Should their adversaries be directly confronted, as the Boston advocates proposed, or should they be led, like Sam's jury, to draw conclusions of their own?

The more militant contingent of "hard" Clams had another, more pointed, complaint. In the context of a democratic, egalitarian organization, the farmers from Montague and certain other "soft" Clams seemed to hold a disproportionate amount of authority. In the often black-and-white political terms of the day, this was considered to be elitism, and the farmers and their allies on the soft side of the debate were accused of engaging, in however well-meaning a way, in the social crime of leadership.

Whatever one may think of this view, it is certainly true that guiding a group is leadership, and that the motives of anyone attempting to influence others could easily be construed to be, in the purest sense, undemocratic. Moreover, a leaderless organization was the standard set by the Clam's founders. It was only later that they discovered how difficult it would be to hew to their earlier ideal.

The final act in this drama occurred late in the spring. In May, as plans for the occupation proceeded along with the debate between hard and soft Clams as to how to conduct it, New Hampshire's attorney general, Thomas Rath, offered a plan of his own that he hoped would satisfy the alliance but avoid the turbulence of the year before. In Rath's proposal, the state would ensure access to the Seabrook site if the Clam would agree to leave it peaceably after a brief weekend occupation.

With opinion already divided within the alliance, no consensus could be reached in response to Rath's proposal. In the breach, with the proposed occupation only a few weeks away, the alliance's central coordinating committee, meeting under considerable stress, made the decision to accept the proposal. On several counts, it coincided reasonably well with the aims of the soft Clams, and so was acceptable to these already influential members of the committee. In an unusual procedural move, however, the committee's announcement of its decision was made before it had been approved by the Clam's all-important constituent local groups. The positive result was a highly successful occupation and alternative energy fair, conducted on the terms offered by the state, in which six thousand Clamshell activists participated. The negative consequence of the committee's action was to undermine its credibility and that of some of its individual members, and to confirm, in the view of the hard Clams, the accusation that the pretense of democracy among the farm-oriented members of the Clam's founding group was merely a convenient screen for a covert form of leadership.

The life of the Clamshell Alliance and the fight against the Seabrook plants continued for another decade. The original reactor was not completed until ten years after its proposed opening date; the second was canceled. Excessive costs forced the owner into bankruptcy. The governor who had supported the project and insisted on a hard line against the Clam lost his bid for reelection. These were not small victories. Montague farmers remained involved in the Clam and the regional fight against nuclear power, but following the debate surrounding the Rath proposal, their roles became somewhat more muted.

By this time, mid-1978, the farm had been for four years the staging ground for local and regional offensives in the battle against nuclear power. The farmers relished their role, and the farm's activist members would continue for years to point out the symbiotic relationship between a supportive life of organic subsistence communal farming at home and the demands of aggressive eco-activism abroad. As 1978 made way for 1979, the year that would bring both the nuclear accident at Three Mile Island and, eerily, its dramatic antecedent in the film *The China Syndrome*, the farmers' notoriety and ability suggested them for a role in yet another, even more comprehensive, effort within this movement in an organization called MUSE.

The National Stage

With the success of the Clamshell Alliance, Green Mountain Post Films, bouts of advocacy journalism, two new books (*No Nukes*, by Anna Gyorgy, and *Energy War*, by Harvey Wasserman), and other farm-related enterprises came new options. Still, of all the things the farmers had done over the past four years, none had quite prepared their extended family for their next act: overseeing five nights of high-profile rock concerts at Madison Square Garden in New York City.

In retrospect, the move from Seabrook to MUSE—Musicians United for Safe Energy—makes eminent sense. At the time, only a few years beyond basic subsistence living, it came as something of a surprise. A success on its own terms, this chapter of continued activism would, like other forays into new territory, come to have a substantial effect on the farm.

MUSE began as the joint effort of concerned popular musicians of considerable stature—Jackson Browne, Bonnie Raitt, Graham Nash, and John Hall among the most committed—to harness their power at the box office to promote important social, environmental, and political issues, including the antinuclear movement. When their sights fell on Madison Square Garden, and the possibility of joint concerts with the capability of generating substantial funding and publicity, they turned to Sam Lovejoy and Harvey Wasserman, and to a lesser extent several other farm-family members, to help plan and execute what would be the

COME HEAR

SAM LOVEJOY

ANTI-NUCLEAR ACTIVIST

"Nuclear Power:
The Unfriendly Atom"

On George Washington's Birthday, 1974, Samuel Holden Lovejoy toppled a 500 foot steel weather tower in Montague, Massachusetts. The tower had been erected by the local utility as part of their project to construct one of the largest nuclear power plants ever planned. Leaving 349 feet of twisted wreckage behind, Lovejoy hitched a ride to the police station where he turned himself in and submitted a four page written statement decrying the dangers of nuclear power and accusing the government and the utility industry of conspiracy and despotism. Six months later, Lovejoy defended his act of civil disobedience in court as "self defense," and was ultimately acquitted of "willfull and malicious destruction of personal property," a five year felony.

Kendall Cram Room / Tulane Univ. Center
TUES. SEPT. 6/77
7:30 pm

A documentary film made in Denmark, which depicts the mechanics of nuclear power plants, will be shown before Lovejoy's address. Learn about the nukes.

Sam on the lecture circuit, 1977. Courtesy FLA.

largest set of events ever in the United States to protest the spread of nuclear power.

The connections were clear. Some of the musicians involved had met Harvey and Sam through support of their work at Seabrook and encountered them in the course of their organizing and talks around the country. Harvey, ever a devotee of the upper levels of activism, had stayed in touch with them. Further ties were forged as the musicians moved among others in their own sphere. Soon, a few scattered concerts in support of antinuclear groups began to jell into a larger effort. As activists and musicians talked more about it, a larger group emerged, now including pop stars James Taylor and Carly Simon. Eventually Graham Nash brought in his immensely well-known peers David Crosby and Stephen Stills, and finally the vastly popular Bruce Springsteen signed on as well. Others joined the effort, but from the beginning, it was clear that a lineup of this strength could fill one of the country's largest venues for days.

Harvey later described this process, which he had followed closely—sealed, he said, over the course of some informal discussions on Martha's Vineyard. As Sam added in another conversation, the founders of MUSE chose him as president to make use of the notoriety and reputation for integrity he had achieved through the tower, as well as the track record in organizing he and Harvey had developed in working with the Clamshell Alliance. They had also distinguished themselves in speaking and organizing nationally for the antinuclear cause.

The planning of the No Nukes concerts entailed the creation of two organizations, one a business to plan and run the events, the other a nonprofit group to give away the proceeds. It required setting up an office in New York, hiring and directing staff, coordinating communication and meetings with the musicians and their agents, fundraising, publicity, design, printing, and numerous other tasks. On top of that it was suggested that a set of record albums be made of the concerts, and then a film as well. All of this required negotiation, contracts, meetings, scheduling, ancillary contractors (recording engineers, filmmakers, caterers, lawyers), and myriad other details.

Even Montague's energetic, devoted activists were tested by this. They learned to commute back and forth on a regular basis. They set up lofts and offices in the city to live and work. They mastered the skills needed both to be effective in the new areas in which they were now working and also to survive, even thrive, in the city. They forged democratic forms of management and acceptable office protocol, and they labored to connect with, while staying independent of, the sectors of straight business and finance with which they now necessarily had to deal.

In some ways, of course, this was a great adventure. Who would have guessed only a few years before that a ragtag group that had fled the city for a simple rural life would return to it on a footing that included salaries, a social network, and high-level connections in the business of pop culture?

On the other hand, the hard work and a high-energy lifestyle took their toll. With looming deadlines, aggressive stakeholders, and large sums of money in play, life at MUSE could become tense. With its many players, it could be hard to manage. With its built-in distance from the farm, it could stretch the lives involved to a fragile point.

The strong egos necessary for such an enterprise were much in evidence, so it's no surprise that conflicts arose that sometimes had lasting effects. One was the rivalry that developed between Harvey and Sam. Harvey had participated in the development of MUSE and felt himself to be one of its essential family. He helped operate the organization and was part of its presence at the New York office. When the critical point was reached in the project—when a credible structure was needed to raise and handle money and a lead figure needed to guide the effort as a whole—Harvey endorsed the choice of Sam for the job of president of MUSE. As Sam himself had pointed out, he was a natural for the position. He was the de facto national leader of the antinuclear movement. He had risked five years in jail to make his point about the planned nuclear plants in Montague, and the Green Mountain Post film based on the tower and the trial, *Lovejoy's Nuclear War*, had proved an effective and wide-ranging organizing tool. His guidance of the Clamshell Alliance had brought great credibility and publicity to the movement. In short, no one could doubt that Sam had his heart in the antinuclear movement and was committed to seeing it expand in a credible, useful way.

Beside this should be placed the parallel career of Harvey. While he had not taken down the tower, he was still living at the farm at the time.

As early local organizing efforts began, both he and Anna Gyorgy, along with others at the farm, had worked with Sam to create a small anti-nuclear movement in western Massachusetts. Harvey later joined the much larger Clamshell effort just a few weeks after it had been conceived and organized in a rudimentary way. He stayed with it through the later divisive struggles that were a turning point for the organization. He had also written a considerable amount about Sam and the antinuclear movement. His articles had appeared in the counterculture magazines *Win* and *Mother Jones*, as well as *The Progressive, The Nation*, and other periodicals, and he was at the time one of the best-known writers in the country on the subject. Like Sam and Anna, he traveled the land speaking, organizing, and demonstrating for the cause.

Those familiar with MUSE in its first years, and with its ties to the farm at Montague, recount that these parallel careers, and claims to importance and authority, came more and more into conflict. Informal discussion in the farm and antinuclear communities suggests that Harvey thought that he would have made a good president of MUSE. Though he credits Sam with doing the best he could under challenging circumstances, he concludes that the tasks to be accomplished by the organization very nearly exceeded the skills that a group of neophytes could muster, and he considers MUSE and its projects lucky to have survived. Sam, for his part, harbors views of his own about Harvey, his abilities, and his methods. While each was widely considered a leader in the movement, the important point here is that their troubled relationship would later have significant ramifications for the life of the farm.

5
New Directions (1983–1992)

By the early 1980s, the farmers had behind them not only their counter-culture history of the Liberation News Service, commune, and political organizing but the concerts, the set of record albums, and the feature film that had resulted from their involvement in MUSE. Equally important to this story, Sam Lovejoy, Dan Keller, Harvey Wasserman, John Wilton, and other farm-family members of the MUSE crew had spent sizable amounts of time in New York and continued to travel, both to the city and around the country, in their efforts to harness their dedication and notoriety to the expansion of the antinuclear cause. New alliances were formed and old ones strengthened or abandoned. Life in the protected hills of Massachusetts and Vermont took on a different cast. Relationships were strained. Accommodations and compromises were made that were unimaginable only a short time before. On the national political scene, perhaps not coincidentally, 1980 marked the beginning of the Reagan era and America's long reaction to the 1960s and to just the sort of people who had always lived on the farm.

As the ground shifted, various changes occurred at the farm in response. One was already apparent: some of the farm's most active and engaged participants had become commuters. Though often paid for their work and thus able to help the farm financially, they spent much less time there. While they injected a spirit of cosmopolitanism into farm life, bringing stories and new friends to the everyday table there, their absence meant that the work of running the farm and maintaining the family atmosphere they loved devolved upon those left behind. It didn't take an economist to see that the same amount of work had to be done by a smaller number of people.

Furthermore, the work of running MUSE and of having become national-level speakers and organizers had taken a toll on the energy of those involved. When they could get back to the farm, their contributions tended to be different than they had been before: practically, they were as much in need of restoring their energy as they were, philosophically, of employing it in support of the community.

Taken together, these circumstances led to a period of friction and discontent, perhaps even malaise, as the farm readjusted, as it had in the early 1970s, to a postactivist life. In conversations with those who were at Montague at the time, this era is often described as one of burnout.

In response to these shifts, individuals re-sorted themselves into changed lives, and new patterns appeared. Sam, as he had always avowed, began to reduce his time in the city with an eye to returning to local organizing in the area, which he did. Still, both for income and to stay in touch with an expanded circle of friends and associates there, he continued to travel back and forth to New York on a regular basis. Harvey, making use of his own wide notoriety, began to forge a career of speaking and writing, as well as consulting to antinuclear and other groups, such as Greenpeace, focused on political, environmental, and social change. Like Sam, he also continued to travel regularly. Anna, who had always taken an interest in feminist issues, began to develop a vocation in that area, eventually leading to the founding of an activist organization of her own.

At the farm itself, this left Tony Mathews, who had taken on the farming, and Janice, who oversaw the garden, to head up most of the physical work that needed to be done. Others were involved, of course, but in view of the future that developed at the farm, these were two of the key figures. The third was Peter Natti. From his wheelchair, he had overseen the building of a woodshop from which he worked successfully both for others and for the farm. He also took on the job of managing the farm's books—its financial records—and continued to do so throughout his time at the farm. Not aspiring to vacations and finding the farm now well suited to his needs, he was there most of the time to help make it run.

The friction and discontent had consequences. In 1982, after a disagreement with Sam, Tony and his future wife, Sue, left the farm, first to move to the neighboring commune of Wendell, and then to set up on their own nearby. In 1983, Harvey, finding his national life impeded by the rural location of the farm, and under pressure from his parents to help them run their business in their later years, returned to his hometown in Ohio. In 1984, Janice began a several-year stint working at a local private school, in part to build a profession, in part so her daughter, Sequoya, could study there. At about the same time, Sam decided to legitimize his reputation for legal savvy by attending law school. In 1986 he and Janice, a couple for more than fifteen years, broke up, leaving the farm without the joint public face for it they had often presented. Nina, who had originally arrived in the Chuckbus with Janice, also left the farm that year for Wendell. Dan and Chuck found themselves very busy with their new business, Green Mountain Post Films, quartered in an old Victorian mansion they had bought from a collapsing cult in a nearby town.

Through these and other changes, the farm often found itself, in the mid-1980s, with only Janice, Sequoya, and Peter Natti in residence. With Janice and Sequoya often away at school, the entire farm and its large house had come to be, in effect, run by a single man in a wheelchair.

Peter will have more to say about this, but the immediate solution to the situation, taken by Janice, was to begin to recruit others to fill in for those no longer present at the farm. Thus began a long string of new residents, sometimes considered farm-family members, at other times something more like renters, who populated the farm for a number of years. Some of these associations worked out; people stayed and contributed to the farm, often for years. Others did not. Throughout this period, a notable quality surfaced in Janice: she liked to have people at the farm, but often she didn't get along with them very well. This trait will reemerge, but the result over this period was an ever-changing cast that had its high and low moments but that, aside from its invitation to move to Montague, often seemed little connected to the farm's original mission or inhabitants. This assessment is not meant to disparage these people or this period. At the time it is simply what the farm was. It is only meant to point out that again the tone of life there had changed.

In the early 1990s, Janice found what she thought was an ideal answer to filling out the needed population at the farm. One of her daughter's former local schoolmates and his wife were serious organic farmers looking for a place to settle down. Attracted by the reputation of the farm as a refuge for a progressive, organic, New Age approach, these neighbors were eager to move in and Janice was glad to have them. Thus arrive on the scene Tim and Lise, a young couple who did solve the immediate problem of populating the farm, but whose later claims on it, and allegiance to particular farm-family members, would become part of the divisive struggle that would trouble Montague in the following years.

Before moving on to this later phase in which a number of the characters encountered here collide with each other in one form or another, it is important to fill in some of their stories more fully, in order to understand how well-meaning community members might develop distinct, even conflicting, views and practices of their own.

Harvey

Of those who ended up determining the long-term history of the farm, certainly Harvey Wasserman was among the first to have joined the community from which it would eventually evolve. As a college student in Michigan and then a graduate student in Chicago, he was part of the early founding and operation of the Liberation News Service in 1967 and 1968. He had known Marshall Bloom briefly during their high-school years and had followed Marshall's career as a budding activist at Amherst, in London, and then at the United States Student Press Association. As a young journalist himself, starting on the *Michigan Daily* in Ann Arbor, and from a visit to Marshall in London, he knew a number of the people in Bloom's growing circle. When LNS took root, first in Washington and then in New York, Harvey commuted to its offices from the Midwest. When Marshall took the news service to the farm in Montague, Harvey, though still respectful of the organization's non-Bloom faction, aligned himself with the group that accomplished the move to western Massachusetts known in farm-family parlance as the heist.

During the farm's first year, Harvey had relocated to New York in order to take a teaching job. He occasionally visited the farm, though for the most part he was based in the city. After the school year, in the summer of 1969, he moved to the farm and began writing his first book, the populist view of American history mentioned earlier. It was published in 1972.

"I loved writing the book at the farm," he told me in 2006.

> Back then, living at Montague Farm was like being in paradise. I mean, it was just the greatest—fantastic. At one point, we had twenty people in that house, so there were always going to be issues. But overall, it was fantastic.
>
> I like to tell people that all the stories they hear about those hippie farms are true. It was just great fun. Also, one of the neat things about the farm was that you could go away. You could go away and come back and it was as if you were never gone. You'd come back and this one was no longer with that one; she was with him, and he was with the other one; that one had left, and this one had come, and, you know, it was all pretty amazing.
>
> For me, the beauty of the farm was overwhelming. I had grown up in suburban Columbus, Ohio, and to live in a place that beautiful was a great privilege. I spent at least an hour, sometimes two hours every day, just walking in the woods. I knew every rock, every tree in the forest in that place. I just couldn't get enough. I watched every sunset every day that I was there on Montague Farm. I watched from a rock I liked up in the field. It was almost genetic. When it got to be four, five, or six in the evening, I was done, I couldn't do anything; I had to go up and sit on the rock.
>
> Then I worked again until two or three in the morning, because that was when we used to lock down the *Michigan Daily* in Ann Arbor. But I never missed a sunset. I must have seen three or four thousand sunsets, and they were all beautiful, every one of them. I used to sleep in the field, you know. It was great to do that. I slept up there a lot, even when it rained. I ruined many a down sleeping bag. I didn't have a tent—there was no need for a tent, really— although I did often wake up dew-soaked in the morning.

Harvey at the farm, 1969. Photo by Peter Simon, courtesy Beech River Books.

Of course, he noted, there were some problems attached to being a writer at the farm:

> I was out there in the garage. I had all my books, on loan—my uncle had a bookstore in Boston—and I was writing about the turn of the century and all this stuff; I was totally in the world of the 1890s. But I would walk into the house and people would be sitting around, and I'd start rapping about the 1890s. Gradually, people would filter out of the room, and I'd be left alone in the kitchen.

Harvey stayed at the farm for fourteen years. He was there at the time of the tower-toppling and the first year of local organizing in the antinuclear cause. After the group's initial success at that, he took a trip of almost a year and a half with his girlfriend of the time, Amy. When he came back in August 1976, the Clamshell Alliance had been formed and was in the midst of its first action in Seabrook. This suited Harvey perfectly

> It was August 1, 1976, and I had just come back from traveling around the world. I mean literally: Amy and I traveled around the world for eighteen months. We were in Hawaii, Japan, Thailand, Malaysia, Singapore, and Indonesia, then we came back up through Singapore and Malaysia. In Indonesia, we spent two months with George, from Wendell Farm. He was doing anthropological work there. It was unbelievably beautiful, just beyond spectacular.
>
> After a week in India, we flew back. We got to Boston on July 31st. I went to a family wedding there, fresh off the plane, and then the next day, August first, I immediately started in with the Clamshell Alliance. I showed up at Seabrook just as they were coming back from the first arrests. I walked in and I immediately became part of the Clamshell Alliance Media Committee.

In Harvey's view, Clamshell, the farm, and LNS—and often other similar organizations—were all related, especially in spirit. "The early Clam was like the early farm," he said. "Everybody was with everybody else."

> It was just kind of a roving commune of people from the six New England states. We'd have these wonderful meetings, they were just

so much fun. We all loved each other so much, you know, and we were all on the same page. It was like the News Service when it first started; we operated on consensus because we could. We didn't have long, drawn-out debates, because we all pretty much agreed on what needed to be done, and how to do it. As with the farm and the News Service, we were mystics. It was to be totally nonviolent. We worked with the Quakers, who are mystics themselves, and we were trained in nonviolence. Nonviolence is a mystical belief. Why should you be able to change the world without violence? What sense does that make? It makes no sense at all, which is why it works.

The early Clam was very much linked to the farm. Dan and Chuck were making the movies. Anna pulled together the *No Nukes* book. I was doing writing and speaking. Tony was organizing. Nina, everybody: Sam, Janice, Janice's friend Karen—Nadja's mom. You know, it was just what we all did, and we didn't think about it. It was just fantastic. We loved all the people we were meeting from New Hampshire. The family just got bigger. And I was going up there to the meetings, and you know—two hours back and forth in my funky Volkswagen. It was just spectacular, it was just wonderful for that first year.

In finding the Clamshell Alliance, as with a number of other things in his life, Harvey's view was that, his hard work aside, he had been very fortunate:

> I mean, talk about being lucky in life, to be able to be part of that, time and again. The early antiwar movement was like that. The early SDS, the early News Service, the early farm, then the early Clamshell. Later, I was lucky enough to get involved in Greenpeace, not at the very beginning but at a time when it was, again, very magical. I joined Greenpeace in 1990. It was so much fun. . . . It was just too much, really. By then, I was older than everybody else, but still, being the resident geezer was great.

This is a list that goes on to considerable length. Ann Arbor in the 1960s, a hotbed of the nascent student movement. The first teach-in, 1965; assaulting the Pentagon from a wheelchair during the March on

Washington, 1967 (he had recently been beaten up at a draft board demonstration in Chicago); Martin Luther King Jr.'s "I Have a Dream" speech
in 1963; JFK campaigning in Ohio in 1960; and, of course, it goes on to
include LNS, the farm, Clamshell, MUSE, and events beyond. It seems
listening to Harvey that during these decades of the protest era, he's
been virtually everywhere at the right time. Even as early as his college
years, he had written an article that was picked up on the national news.
Suddenly he was on the airwaves as a spokesman for the new generation.

He was also a writer and a scholar; he had been in Chicago on a Wood-
row Wilson Fellowship. He saw himself as an intellectual with a clear philosophy. The LNS split provides a good example. The breaking point for
him, he said, had come when the non-Bloom faction had insisted on editing
everyone's work. The press was no longer to be free, but guided by political correctness. This went against Harvey's First Amendment principles
and shifted him to the more cultural, permissive side of the News Service's
ideological divide. Similarly, in the Clamshell debate, he had remained on
the side of the "soft" Clams, advocating a nonviolent, principled approach
that bolstered the sort of viable long-term political strategy he believed in.

It's clear to anyone who meets him that Harvey loves what he does. "I
guess I was just born to be an activist," he once said to me. "I love doing
this stuff. It doesn't pay very well, but as they say, the work is steady."

Along with this goes a style of enthusiasm and exuberance that can be
experienced either as joyous or as a form of indomitable energy, depending
on one's relation to it. Certainly Harvey's own view is the former, though
when roused, he is well able to summon the other side of his personality.

And he does have another side. At LNS, though he moved to the farm,
Harvey attempted for a long time to reconcile the two factions in the dispute, believing strongly, and almost alone, that the news service would
be more effective as a single unit. At the farm, he introduced a strain of
militant vegetarianism. In the Clamshell conflict, he was instrumental in
pushing through and then announcing the organization's controversial
response to the Rath proposal. At MUSE, he had sparred with Sam over
issues of management and finance.

In the course of describing his involvement with activism, he had
made a remark that caught my attention. "I joined Greenpeace in 1990,"
he said. "It was so much fun. You know, to be involved in an organization

that has a navy! It was just too much, really." Having a navy (Greenpeace), having an army (the Pentagon march, the Clamshell Alliance)—it would not be a great step, later, to having an attorney.

Sam

Like Harvey, Sam Lovejoy was a highly principled veteran of the wars of social change. In college, from 1964 to 1969, he had had what he called in an interview in 2008 "an open room," "an open social life." Friends and acquaintances were free to stop by, listen to his records, lounge a bit, cool out, have a smoke, even if he wasn't there. He saw himself as part of the great wave of change that characterized the 1960s, the era of "sex, drugs, and rock 'n' roll," as he often puts it. "I was, in a way, kind of a social ringleader," he said.

And, like Harvey's, his history went far back, all the way to high school. At the private school he had attended as a day student, near his home in Springfield, Massachusetts, he had taken the first steps to organize a strike in favor of student rights. The strike was subverted by insiders on the school staff, but in short order the document he had questioned had been rewritten to give the students the rights Sam thought they should have—and to give him a key position in the new political order.

He had a similar experience in college, when a plan to take over a building in the service of progressive views was carefully manipulated by the administration to avoid student action by ceding some, but only some, of the demands they had made. Both experiences left Sam with a taste for success and public life, but also a deep suspicion of the danger of complicity and co-option. In his college years he had also briefly been the head of New England SDS, and had come to care so much about social change that he had switched his major from math and physics to political science.

"I was politically even with these folks," he said about the farm in the same interview, "so moving to a commune was sort of thrilling to me. It was just another step in my own political-cultural attitude."

Sam moved to the farm in the spring of 1969, near the end of his senior year. Over the summer he got to know Marshall, whom he had met only briefly before. He admired what he saw as Marshall's single-minded devotion to the farm and was impressed, in this summer of cucumbers, candles, and our first garden, with the notion he attributes to Marshall that the farm should be self-sufficient.

Deep emotional involvement and belief in self-sufficiency were but two of the ways in which Sam was aligned with the farm. He was an activist, as evidenced by his political adventures in high school and college. He was socially aware, as is made clear in his sharing his room and belongings with others. He was egalitarian, fighting for the rights of other students, and antiauthoritarian—at one point he had been expelled from college for not completing required courses, although, as he explained, he could do the work perfectly well, he just didn't think, for his own reasons, that he should be compelled to do it.

All of this was in some measure characteristic of its time. But Sam had another connection to the farm as well. Little known to most of the farmers, he had been helping to support them. In the can-do, entrepreneurial mode he had developed early on, he had established several businesses while still in college, some purely commercial, some with more altruistic, countercultural leanings. (Some of his friends at the time called him Magic Sam.) When his friend Irv, who had been living at the farm, turned to him to help raise money for the farm's mortgage, he deftly executed a deal that netted the needed sum. He also reached into his own pocket to help purchase our first farm equipment. When he moved to the farm, he employed some of the farmers in his house-painting and other businesses. Thus began a long pattern of financial involvement, as Sam reinforced his views about the farm through regimes of his own devising.

Later in the year, in the late fall of 1969, Sam was among those from the farms who participated in the Venceremos Brigades to Cuba, the SDS-related project to help Cubans harvest the endangered sugar crop. When he returned, he says, weeks after Marshall's death in early November, it was to help fulfill Marshall's dream for the farm, as he understood it. Originally he had been planning an extended stay in Latin America; instead, he came home.

At that time, he said in his 2008 interview, "I thought the most important thing for my life was to come back to the farm, stabilize the commune, work my ass off to make the farm be a farm, and maintain our politics."

This is where the long-term farm adventure begins for Sam. When he looks back, it is from this point that he dates most of the precepts he takes to be axiomatic about his relation to it. Among these are its self-sufficiency and, as much as possible, independence from the larger economic, financial, and social system; strong ties to the land, as the source of the self-sufficiency; and integration with the local community—as he puts it, "There won't be a revolution unless you can actually communicate with your neighbor." For these reasons, Sam maintained the farm as his base of operations even when his work kept him away a good deal of the time, and in order to do that, he made sure the farm itself was maintained so that it could fill that role.

This last mission involved several other aspects of his philosophy. Sam believed in communal life itself and spent considerable effort rallying farm members to move themselves onto "the same page," as he, like Harvey, often expresses it. Similarly, he believed that leadership was best exercised not as a long-term privilege but in brief, specific, case-related bursts.

"I have always been opposed to leadership in the permanent sense," Sam told his interviewer. "I think people arise in a situation and their ideas or their position attract a following. What screws it up is that the leader then wants to hang onto it. So I believe that leaders should be only a momentary event. You do need someone to ultimately make some decisions," he admitted. "If the group empowers them to make those decisions, all to the good. But that leadership—give it up as fast as possible."

In a similar vein, as we can see from the tower incident and the statement connected with it, Sam believed in symbolic action. In his view, the farm, with its grassroots approach and ties to larger activism, was a beacon illuminating what could be done by citizens themselves in service to social and political change. For this reason, too, he felt it important to keep the farm functioning and fruitful.

On top of such views were layered some of Sam's own traits and personal beliefs. He may not have believed in leadership, but he often found himself a leader, or at least working in some form to shape the farm and the other organizations he became involved in. This disjunction often led to a behind-the-scenes approach that avoided acknowledging his true role and allowed him to deny the ego involvement associated with most leadership.

This suited another side of Sam. A New Englander through and through, and—perhaps not insignificantly—raised in the haunts of the radical cleric Jonathan Edwards, he was a reformer with a strong interest in ethical behavior. Denying personal involvement allowed him additional moral stature and the chance to reframe his leadership as community service. The important issues in which he involved himself raised the stakes even higher. Who was going to argue with someone whose motives were to protect the farm family, connect it to the community, work its land to support it, and weigh in on some of the world's most difficult problems?

The obverse of this latter-day New England virtue was the sort of authoritarianism that only a devoted antiauthoritarian can muster. If pressed, Sam would admit that he was related to Elijah Lovejoy, a celebrated abolitionist who died for his extreme beliefs. (As a matter of principle, Sam would never encourage such flattering comparisons.) Armed with a similarly weighty moral message, Sam didn't mind taking extremes himself. In a much earlier interview, when he was still at MUSE, I had asked him, given the complexity of the world's problems and the difficulty of solving them, what about shortcuts? What about a dictator holding a population hostage, poor and unfed, for his own needs? Pull the plug, said Sam matter-of-factly. But, the Realpolitik side of him added, such difficulties rarely reside entirely in individuals. It wouldn't be the right action to take, since it probably wouldn't solve the problem.

Sam's character is not a secret. A gregarious, entertaining storyteller, he will be the first to regale listeners with his life and adventures; others soon add tales of their own. In the area of social engineering, he will tell you that in college he joined a traditional fraternity—the "animal house" of the Amherst campus—but untraditionally first cajoled its members toward the new ways of thinking and acting of those times (a few well-placed joints helped), and then persuaded them to abolish themselves in favor of a much more open and liberal organization. The research, advocacy, and procedural skills exhibited in this stratagem bear the strong marks of Sam's style. Its results reflect his social and political views. How grateful other brothers were for this accomplishment is not known.

As an inspired user of tools, he will explain that his single share of stock in Northeast Utilities, the corporation behind the planned nuclear plants in Montague, was one of the best purchases he ever made, entitling him to the company's annual reports and invitations to meetings that were very helpful in his quest to subvert the enterprise in which he had nominally invested. Similarly, he once told me that if he could use the stock market or commodities exchange to raise money for the antinuclear cause, he would be happy to do it, even though such financial organizations run entirely counter to the sort of social ideals he espouses. In his later life as an attorney, often defending causes in which he believed, he alerted me to the realities of advocacy practice. You don't want to get in our way, he warned; we'll try anything.

These were skills and beliefs Sam applied to the farm at Montague. He envisioned the farm as a base for social action, and from the time he returned from Cuba, as he recounts it, all his effort before the tower, and a good deal of it after, was devoted to creating and maintaining a viable, independent foundation for social change. In his 2008 interview he said:

> We needed a financial base, a home, a taproot from which we could then spring. That the farm became a stable agricultural and financial unit, a home, gave us the freedom and the love . . . to feel like you could go out, change the world yet again, or to work on an issue that was going to help change the world, [make it] a better place, and be able to fall back on the thing that was sustaining you.
>
> By 1972, we had pulled it off. We had figured it out. We had gotten the equipment. We could milk the cows—we had a couple cows. The barn was fixed up enough so we could deal with that. The fences were patched. The pastures were fenced in. The crop cycle was working. The garden was about an acre—an organic, unbelievable thing.

In Sam's view, others were expected to embrace this work:

> I was very insistent that people who lived there reach out into the community, get to know community people, and that those community people were inevitably going to be contacts we were going to need, if for no other reason than practical. You get to know the gas-station guy because you buy gas from him and he might be able

to help you find used tires for two dollars apiece, rather than having
to buy new ones, . . . or if a car broke down, because we only had one
car that worked. And then the store guy and the tractor-parts guy.
Just don't be paranoid of these people; they're going to become our
friends. So that was an attitudinal change that I felt very strongly
about. I was basically the outreach person in a lot of ways, particularly in the beginning.

"I was very insistent"; "I felt very strongly"; For Sam, these would
always be the important criteria. People needed to be "on the same page,"
as he had earlier encouraged. Perhaps what he called "educating" them
might help—and probably it would. Still, it's notable that in Sam's mind,
it was his own principles and vision that ought to prevail. "It's a commune, we're all sharing," he asserted. "And a lot of the fights I would get
into were with people who were not sharing as much as me.

"If you've got a dream, you can work on a dream," he said, invoking words from the movement out of which the farm had evolved in the
1960s. "For me—and I can only specifically talk about me—the farm was
a political statement. I was willing to share all of my income, and I was
willing to share all of my energy, I only wanted other people to have that
same dream."

"The way I look at it, it's liberated territory," he had said to me with
some finality about the farm, back in his MUSE days.

"It'll never slide back?" I asked, always on watch for a reality check.

"Can't," he said.

Janice

One reason Sam was convinced of the farm's security, even in the uncertain times it faced during the Reagan era and after, was the relationship
he had developed with Janice. She had arrived at the farm about a year
after Sam, with the Chuckbus group (see chapter 3). Before long the two
of them were a couple. Besides their personal relationship, Sam took on
informally but very seriously the role of second parent to Janice's daughter, Sequoya, a matter to which he called attention in his tower statement
to make the case for the humanitarian importance of his act: "I'd fallen in

Janice (*right*) and Nina (*center*) at a farm meeting. Photo by Emmanuel Dunand, courtesy FLA.

love with a beautiful four-year-old girl named Sequoya, who lives on the farm," he wrote. "She and all the children, and their children's children yet unborn, depend on us, they are innocents. They depend on us not to desecrate the environment, trees, and rivers, all in the name of gross profit. I knew I had to do it for Sequoya."

Over the next two decades, the family trio of Sam, Janice, and Sequoya would often come to represent the steadiest public face of the farm. Janice, through most of this period, was living at the farm and a key figure in running it. Sam, even when he was not there, was viewed as the second half of her team (or vice versa), always available for help, support, and advice. Sequoya, the first child to live at the Montague farm, became a lead member of the next generation to care for and care about the farms.

Janice's first years at the farm were those of our basic adjustment to rural life. She proved an able gardener and contributed energetically to the many tasks that involved us all, from repairing and redecorating the farmhouse, to care of the livestock we were quickly accumulating, to shaping the new dietary, canning, and cooking habits that came to define life in the kitchen, in many ways the center of activity in the house. Beyond this, she was also, of course, raising her daughter, one of the small but lively group of children growing up on the farms at that time. During this period, the garden grew to be a flourishing staple of our lives, the house considerably more comfortable, the kitchen better, if not perfectly, ordered (this was, after all, a bastion of alternative life), and her daughter to be the delightful four-year old Sam had spoken of in his statement on the tower.

Like many at the farm, Janice was away at times. Among them, as she recalled not long ago, was a brief stint in Cambridge, Massachusetts, with Sam in the early 1970s, and a visit to farm friends in Seattle during 1972–73. (It was in connection with returning to Montague from a visit to her in Seattle that Sam often recounts first seeing the tower in 1973.) Mostly, though, she and Sam were a strong presence at the farm during its first fifteen years. Even then, after they broke up, they remained a joint force there for nearly another decade and a half.

Among the events of the years leading up to the farm reunion in 1993 related to Janice, we have already followed two: the tower-toppling in 1974 and the Seabrook campaign, 1976–78, both, of course, tied closely to Sam. Earlier on there was the arrival of Anna Gyorgy, who would be a longtime colleague of Janice's at the farm and in its larger community, as well as in the antinuclear movement that came to take center stage there. A little later, in 1976, through Anna, Peter Natti arrived for his twenty-year stay at the farm, a period during which he and Janice would be, at different times, both adversaries and allies. During this time, Janice also began her career in the health field, first in the mid-1970s with the founding of a health center in the nearby town of Greenfield, and later in connection with the local private school where she was working. (Eventually, in the mid-1990s, she began a new phase of this work with a move to Colorado, to which she continues to commute each year.)

In the late 1970s and early 1980s came the period when Sam and others were often in New York, or traveling, in connection with MUSE and the larger antinuclear movement, leaving Janice and Peter to become the de facto keepers of the farm. In 1986, factors related to this regimen of separate lives led Janice and Sam's breaking up. (Harvey, also involved in the farm's new geographically extended life, tells a similar personal tale.) From 1984 to 1988, as mentioned above, Janice taught nutrition at the school Sequoya was attending. Finally, in 1992, as mentioned earlier, came the arrival of Tim and Lise, the neighboring organic farmers Janice recruited to help fill the void of full contributing members; during the following ten years they would play a key role in the life of the farm.

Janice's tenure at the farm—the longest of anyone in its history—and her relation to Sam, whose involvement was of equal intensity and, though often at a distance, of virtually equal length, constitute one of the central conundrums of its life. At bottom, there seem to be two principal factors involved, one stemming from Janice, the other from Sam. Once Janice moved to the farm she increasingly considered it her home, and over the years, this developed, in her view, from the kind of circumstance that had brought most of its extended family to the farm into something more approaching a right of ownership. This left others to wonder: Does longevity or tenure equal ownership? Or, equally compelling from the point of view of Janice and others who put considerable time and resources into the farm: Doesn't investment lead to ownership? And while there was no doubt that Janice, in tending and at times guiding the farm, was helping to sustain its existence—often a difficult task, to be sure—her personal approach to that work and her apparent lack of an overall strategy or philosophy comparable to those of the farm's earlier years left her with little authority over its life other than that derived from her accumulated experience living there.

This is where Sam came in. Sam, with his view of the farm as a base for social action and a beacon for change, provided the ideological grounding Janice needed to support her governance of the farm. While they remained a couple, this combination went largely unquestioned. It was a symbiotic relationship that from each of their individual points of view worked very well. Absent Sam, however, after 1986, or even before, as the situation at the farm became increasingly rocky, Janice—a high school graduate without the background in social science, politics, economics, or the other resources farm members sometimes brought to the communal table, a young mother who had fled her earlier conventional life to embark on a primal New Age experience in the woods of Vermont—was ill-equipped to take on the demands that had fallen to some of the farm community's earlier gifted leaders (or, as they would probably prefer to be called, de facto leaders)—Marshall, Cathy, Sam, and Susan of Montague; Raymond and Verandah of Packer Corners; Dan Keller of Wendell Farm.

The solution to this configuration of events—the need for a home in combination with the need to continue the farm's larger political and social mission beyond the activities of its individual members (Janice was, after all, involved *personally* in the health and antinuclear movements, even if she was not an acknowledged leader)—resulted in continued ties between Janice and Sam. Even after breaking up, even after Sam moved a considerable amount of his life to New York to direct the MUSE organization, even after he married someone else, even after he bought a house of his own in town, some two miles from the farm, and even after Janice began spending substantial spans of time in Colorado, she and Sam continued to be a force at the farm and together to support her rights, approaching ownership, to various portions of the farm and its life. Clearly, looking at the history, it suited them each, both separately and together, to assume the mantle of the farm.

In addition to these larger matters, there was the issue of Janice's manner with others. In her view she was coping over the years with the difficult situations that arose in communal life, and with the many varied people it attracted. Most in the farm family, I think, have considerable sympathy for this outlook on a set of circumstances many of them had experienced themselves. But over the long period she lived at the farm, a distinct picture emerged of Janice staying her course while numerous communards, long term or short, came and went. Other women were apparently especially vulnerable. One long-time farm resident said simply that for Janice, the farm was home and that others would come to be viewed by her as intruders. "Strong women not getting along in the kitchen," was the way this syndrome was expressed. The strongest of these would turn out to be Lise.

Peter

So far, the stories followed here might be characterized as of a generally positive nature that on closer inspection turn out to have some troubling implications. For a number of those who passed through the farm, though, it was often the reverse, a difficult history that found grounds for positive expression at the farm. One of the most poignant of these is the story of Peter Natti. In October 2006, ten years after he had left, I went to see him at his home in Gloucester, Massachusetts, to talk about his years at the farm. He told me how he had gotten to Montague. "It was in 1976," he said. "I took a ride out to western Massachusetts with my cousin Isabel, a friend of Anna's, to see this place we'd heard of. We met all the people there. It was really an amazing spot. A week later, I moved in."

> It was desperation on my part. I had to get out of here. I was in a car accident in 1973, a head-on car crash, broke my neck; paralyzed; eleven months in a hospital in recovery, and then a year in Florida sort of in a daze recovering. When I came back from Florida, in the spring, I had to get out of Gloucester—just couldn't stay. I was living under the roof of my parents. It was too painful all around. I needed to recover my independence. The farm presented an opportunity, and I just jumped in.

The recovery—it was like anything else; you go through all the stages, you know, all the emotions: denial, "why me?" and all the rest of it. But in Florida I realized that that wasn't the way I wanted to spend the years of my life, so I moved back here, and was looking for something to give me direction. It turned out that the farm really gave me that direction.

I was always a worker, growing up. My father instilled in me the value of work. He just made work fun, so I could never keep still. If I would go to a beach, I'd build a sand castle; I just couldn't sit on the beach and do nothing. My father was the principal of the high school here, so for me that was quite an interesting four years. His career was in school administration, but his passion was pottery. He used to putter around here in his pottery studio and work the land. He taught me how to do ceramics at an early age, and, you know, cutting and splitting wood, splitting stone, planting, fishing.

So I had that background. At the farm, it sort of jelled, because I was really looking for a vocation after my accident. I tried pottery, but in pottery I would get to a certain point and I couldn't complete it myself. I would have to have help. I wanted to find a job that I could do from start to finish myself.

At the farm, at first I lived down in the garage for four years. I took one corner of that room and made a little workbench, and I just started repairing things. It was one of those great combinations: the farm needed things done and I needed to do things. That started me off. The first winter I lived there, all I did, basically, was to patch up broken windows.

This surprised me. I reminded him that by 1976 people had been at the farm for eight years. "Oh," he said, "there was cracked and broken glass all over the place. The house was a sieve. I can remember sitting in the kitchen right next to the woodstove, the little cook stove, and being a foot away from it, and if you turned around, you could see your breath in the air. For years, we'd have to start a fire in the dining room an hour before dinner, just so the room would be warm." Before long, Peter's work had expanded and so had his shop:

It started out with repairing window sashes, and then I went on to fixing doors and trying to make the house tighter. Then I started doing other things. I made a dining-room table. That's when Albert Miolatasi was living there and he took on the job of repairing the barn. On one wing of the barn, I guess they had torn the roof off a year or two years before with the idea of repairing it, but they never got around to doing it. It was going to ruin the whole barn, so Albert decided he'd take that on as a project. When he got through redoing the barn and the roof, we took one section of it and made a shop. That was the start of the main shop out at the farm.

Over the twenty years I was there, it came together. Two or three years later, I took over another bay, and then a few years after that, expanded into another. It just sort of grew from there. I got more and more work, and all of a sudden, I was not just fixing things for the farm, I was actually doing projects for other people and making money, so it turned into a great vocation.

It was fun to go out there and do things. What I liked about the farm was that I saw that as a communal shop. I know that my friend Dennis used to love to come down and do projects there, and our neighbor Peter, every time I see him, he always says "God, you know those days at the farm were the best days"—his farm liked to be able to come down and use the shop. I mean, everybody just came in and used it. Sam was always using it.

That's what I do down here now, in Gloucester. I have a wood-working shop and a lot of different people come and use it. That's just my philosophy, you know—if you have something, share it.

He certainly did have a shop to share. In the Lanesville section of Gloucester, where he lives in a wing of his family's old house next to one of the area's distinctive abandoned quarries, Peter has an entire building fitted out for his use. Sawdust, clamped pieces of matching board, and other signs of work are evident everywhere. Outside, he has a computer-run sawmill, so that from his wheelchair he can produce the wood he needs for cabinetry or saw up lumber for sale. Just in the brief time I was there, several people came by to use the facilities he had set up.

He went on to tell me his view of communal life at the farm:

My whole thing was you come in and you give what you want to give, and don't expect anything back, because, communally, that's how you have to work. When I first moved there, it was just amazing to have this huge organic garden. There was a milk cow. We wound up doing our own chickens, our own turkeys, the whole maple-syrup deal, honey bees. It was perfect self-sufficiency, and I think that's what Marshall and Raymond were originally trying to do—get back to the land.

In 1976, there were fourteen people living there, three kids and eleven adults. It was just amazing to get thrown into this mix, coming from a situation where I had pretty much been living by myself.

At the time Peter moved there, Montague was just gearing up for the Seabrook era, a period he remembers well:

That was my political awakening, moving to the farm. It was really eye-opening to get swept up into that whole antinuclear movement. It was dynamic, it was really amazing being around the farm at that time. That was in 1976, you know, when it started, so we just got right into it. We did a lot of traveling up to Seabrook and meeting with the people up there. It was really great having all these different people from the antinuclear movement around the world actually stopping into the farm.

I remember one time during the whole Seabrook thing when we had a busload of Japanese peaceniks drive into the yard. They had heard about the farm. I think Harvey had been speaking over there, and so about thirty Japanese came out of the bus with two translators, and it was just like—that's the kind of stuff that would happen. People would show up out of the blue. We had a great afternoon. Tony [Mathews] went down and got a couple cases of beer. We went out to the garden and got a huge meal together. It was the first time the Japanese had actually loosened their ties and taken off their jackets. For the next couple of weeks, we got thank-you letters saying that that was the high point of their trip.

Another time we had a different Japanese guy come up to the farm. He had hitchhiked across the country. He had read one of the books on the farms, maybe one of Raymond's that had been translated over there. He showed up and he didn't speak any English

The German edition of Steve Diamond's *What the Trees Said*. Courtesy FLA.

The Japanese edition of Ray Mungo's *Cosmic Profit*. Courtesy FLA.

at all, but he spent ten days with us. It was all sign language, you know, and doing stuff together. There was another, a German kid who showed up one time. He had read *What the Tree Said* in German and came to this country and thumbed up from New York to Montague just to see the farm.

People would just say, "Okay I'm going there." That was the stuff that would happen a lot. People would just show up and want to spend time. That's why it was so much fun.

Mood Shift

These stories reflected Peter's early days at Montague. But he recalled that as Seabrook and MUSE had wound down, and the farm moved into its next era, life there had shifted into another key:

Well, you know, Sam and Harvey were heavily involved in MUSE. Harvey would make periodic visits to the farm, and it was great, but we all knew that that was his life at the time: being on the road, writing, doing lectures. That was Sam's thing, too, and the people who were there at the time, Janice and myself and whoever else, we just took on the responsibility of keeping the farm going. It never really bothered me that they weren't there all the time to help out.

Sure, there was a lot of tension with people being gone, and throwing the responsibility onto the people who were left there, but what are you going to do? You just do as much as you can. If people harbored resentment, that was their issue, not mine.

When they came back, they helped; when they weren't there, we just did as much as we could. If the hay needed to be brought in, somehow it got done. I mean somebody would show up on a weekend and they'd say, "Hey let's go grab the truck and bring in the hay," and it would get done—"the magic," as we used to say.

By Sequoya's junior year, though, I think it was, everybody else had sort of left the farm for one reason or another and there was just Janice, myself, and Sequoya. They were gone all day at school, so there I was by myself taking care of the place. It was tough. I'm trying to keep a seventeen-room farmhouse heated for three people, and basically what I did all day long was tend the fires.

By that time, there were ramps and I could go back and forth to the shop. After I'd been there a few years and they realized I was going to stay, we did that. On days when I couldn't take the chance of getting stuck, I would stay in the house. But most of the time I could get out to the shop and back, so I still put in my time out there. But you know, again, it was just one of those situations. It would have been great to have more help, but it wasn't there. It was my home, though. That's the way you have to look at it. I always considered the farm my home, and you do anything you can for your home.

Gone were the dynamism, livestock, and lamp-lit dinners of earlier years, I noted. "Oh yeah," he said; "everything just shriveled up. There was no one around to do it."

And what of Sam and Harvey when they were at the farm? "Well, Sam, you know, really likes to be the center of attention," he went on. "He was a great storyteller; I loved to hear him. But people would come

Peter Natti at Seabrook, 1977. Photo by Eric A. Roth, courtesy FLA.

to visit and he would go down memory lane, the tower and all that. He would do that all the time. And Janice and I would be thinking: *The corn needs to be brought in and he's holding court.* At some point, you just have to stop talking about what you did and *do* something."

For the people at the farm, Harvey had his blind spots as well. "Harvey seemed to have a hollow leg," Peter said with a smile.

> We'd all sit around, there would be ten people there at the dinner table, and everybody would have their meal, and everybody else would have maybe a little bit of seconds, and then Harvey would sit there and every evening he would say, "Does anybody want any more?" And whatever else was left on the table, he would proceed to consume.
>
> I know he has an incredible metabolism, and likes to work into the early morning hours, but sometimes that caused a little resentment. If there was enough there for a second evening, the cooks all of a sudden are saying to themselves, "Well, I could put this away and I won't have to cook tomorrow night, or I can leave it on the table and Harvey will eat it all."
>
> He would blow in all of a sudden, like a whirlwind. He'd talk about this, and talk about that, and he'd say "Here's what needs to be done around the farm." When he was at the farm, you know, he would definitely focus in to find out what was going on. Then he'd do a little thing, and he'd just disappear out the door again. And it was, like the old days on TV: "Who was that masked man, and why does he come here?"

Overall, though, Peter's view of his life at the farm, especially in light of its upcoming turmoil, was extremely positive, and really exemplary of its best values:

> I didn't actually get access to the farm, for me to be able to get in and out of the main house, wheelchair accessible, for two years. When I first moved out there and went into town, with all the curbs, you know, I couldn't get around. I can remember being hauled up to Packer Corners to go to their New Year's Eve party, and it was fun, but I had to get towed around through snow banks and pulled in backwards and it turned out to be quite an adventure.

But I tell you, the day I could get in and out of the farm by myself was a great day, it was amazing. It was liberating. All of a sudden, I could go to the house or to my shop any time I wanted to, I didn't have to wait for somebody to be there to bounce me down the stairs. It was just like: Wow!

The farm gave me my life back. And as far as having something to motivate me, when I finally got into the woodworking, it was just great. I'd work seven days a week. Monday through Friday I'd work for paying jobs. Saturday I'd work on stuff around the farm. Sunday was left if I wanted to go out and do something for myself. So I'd be out in the shop literally all the time.

He was happy to do it, he said.

Some people at the farm seemed to expect a 50/50 return. It doesn't work that way; you know, communally, it just doesn't. I took my whole disability check and I stuck it in the farm account every month. It was just gone. It was like, "This is communal money; boom, there it goes."

I figured at one point that between money and renovations, I had probably put eighty or ninety thousand dollars into the farm over twenty years. That was a lot of money, but as I said, it was my home. When I moved there, I never expected anything back. This isn't a place you're going to get a retirement fund out of, and that's what I liked about it. That's not why we did this thing. If people go in there and don't want to put sweat equity into the place, you know, maybe they shouldn't live communally.

And what of the others, as the reunion approaches, who would play active roles in the future of the farm? By the early 1990s, Cathy Rogers had long ago returned to Seattle and become a physician. Michael Curry had completed graduate school and was beginning a career on the faculty of UCLA. John Wilton, who had left the farm to study music, returned to his first calling, visual design, and had begun what would become a long tenure in a cramped apartment in Greenwich Village, though he did continue with music as a strong avocation. Also in New York was Susan

Mareneck, who was living with her two children in a loft in Tribeca and making her way in the world of teaching and art. Our farm mate Irv, now an attorney, lived just off Broadway, not far away. Susan's former husband, John Anderson, had become a doctor. Harvey had moved back to Columbus and Steve Marsden to his native Iowa. Steve Diamond had permanently relocated to California. Anna Gyorgy had married and was living at the various foreign diplomatic posts held by her German husband. Lazarus Quon could not be located. It was commonly thought that given his propensity for bold, precipitous living, and in the new era of AIDS, he might have died.

Among those still in the area, Sam was busy in his new role assisting in the conservation of land. Tony and his wife, Sue, were building and teaching a few miles north of the farm. Dan and Chuck were growing their film business. Janice, along with the newly arrived Tim and Lise, was still at the farm.

By this point, the life of the farm, both in itself and as an avatar of other sixties-era countercultural communities, had become quite complex. With all of this activity, and some new players on the stage, the scene was set for the farm's twenty-fifth-year reunion.

6

The Reunion (1993)

The farm's celebration of its twenty-fifth year, a milestone unimaginable during its hardscrabble early days, took place in Montague in August of 1993. Those attending included some forty earlier residents, their children, friends, neighbors, the farm's extended family, and, of course, those currently living there.

Over the period of years since its founding—years that stretched from the last months of Lyndon Johnson and the dark days of Richard Nixon, through the flickering but disappointing administration of Jimmy Carter, back to the reactive regime of Ronald Reagan, and now again to the hopeful days of the early Clinton years—Montague Farm had developed roughly as outlined in the preceding chapters. Some viewed the farm as relatively secure, an island of New Age culture and a stage for social change where living a simple life on the land was possible. Others saw it as unstable and, despite its successes, unable to evolve into a reliable community with clarity of governance and consistent expectations for those living there.

With the recent arrival of Tim and Lise, neighbors-turned-residents, a new series of issues had arisen—really an old set revisited. The new residents had taken to the farm in a strong way, and thus presented a challenge to its existing order and those supporting it, especially Janice and Sam. To neighbors and friends, it was clear that the long-standing

Preparations for the farm reunion, 1993. Photo by Laurie Cohen, courtesy FLA.

debate over who belonged at the farm and who would manage it was continuing in another guise, destabilizing it and threatening its future.

With such questions in the air and new residents of uncertain status yearning for a larger role, much time had been spent before the reunion preparing for meetings that would help set the future direction of the farm. Amid a colorful weekend of teepees, cookouts, music, and family folklore, large conclaves met in the expansive spaces of the barn to discuss finances, ownership, and appropriate stewardship of the farm's substantial holdings of buildings and land. The mood was positive. The family's newly minted attorneys offered counsel. The community worked together, and in the end, though not officially signed, a reasonable compact was devised and agreed to by all. The weekend was memorable, and most in the farm family left feeling that the future of their shared heritage—and a flagship of generational idealism—was assured.

To fill in the full dimensions of these meetings, some additional background will be helpful. Over the past few years before the reunion, concern had been mounting among neighbors and the larger farm community over what the farm properly represented and how best to pursue such ideal political or philosophical principles as could be found there in practical real-world terms that all could agree on. Discussion had taken place through e-mails, phone calls, letters, meetings, and visits. The first and most basic of these issues was: *Who owns the farm?*

The Trust

At Marshall's death on November 1, 1969, he left the farm to a trust designated, in the characteristically sardonic jargon of the farm, the Fellowship of Religious Youth, a wholesome name he hoped would help reduce outside scrutiny of our lives. The group he named to oversee it was made up of seven of those living on the farm at the time—Michael Curry, Steve Diamond, Steve Marsden, Cathy Rogers, James Tapley (Laz), Harvey Wasserman, and John Wilton. How Marshall arrived at this configuration was never determined; by the time it was discovered in his brief, hand-typed will, its author was no longer available to clarify the details.

The generally accepted explanation of the formation of the trust, often shortened simply to its initials, FRY, was that this group constituted in

Marshall's view a sound, competent core of citizens of the farm capable of conducting its business and of making whatever future decisions might be necessary to guide its health and well-being. Others lived there at the time, and certainly the extended family of the farm offered additional candidates who might have served as trustees, but aside from some informal second-guessing, the makeup of the board of trustees of the Fellowship of Religious Youth was never seriously questioned. To most in the community, though there were many ways of parsing it, it was as reasonable a choice as any. Considering that the group was composed in the last hours of the life of a young man bedeviled by unfathomable contradictions and fears, and that it had lasted unchanged for some twenty-five years, one could conclude, by the time of the reunion, that its purpose as envisioned had probably been remarkably well served.

Having recovered somewhat from the shock of Marshall's death and begun to find our way again, the next step was to translate Marshall's expressed wishes into a legal document. There were, after all, not only our idealistic goals and chosen way of life at stake but a property and buildings viewed as being of some value by the world outside our doors. Over the course of 1970, members of the designated trust, especially Steve Diamond, a founder of the farm, worked with a Boston lawyer who had known Marshall to craft the Fellowship of Religious Youth Realty Trust. It was finished by the end of the summer of that year. This document, signed and filed in 1973, confirmed the makeup of the board and set out in fifteen articles the structure, operation, and goals of the organization. This was a logical and necessary development, but as a step along the path of legal and philosophical life of the farm, it is worth noting that at this stage the farm and the trust moved, as entities on paper, from five lines in a personal document of half a page to a formal instrument of some 140 lines filling five legal-sized sheets. As contracts go, this may be small; the interests and responsibilities it codified, however, would loom relatively large.

In 1980, thirteen years before the reunion, when it was set to expire, the trust had been renewed. On February 1, 2001, some seven and a half years after the reunion, it would be due for either further renewal or expiration.

As to those overseeing the trust, the outlook of its officers can best be described as benign neglect. Before long most of the trustees had left the farm, and within a dozen years, all of them. They remained friends and kept in informal touch both with each other and the larger farm family. The farm itself, rather than being governed by the board, instead continued along its path largely guided by those living there. Residents paid taxes and the mortgage and kept up the farm physically, including renovations and additions. Trustees would occasionally visit or write, but on both sides of this arrangement, less was considered more. Residents wanted not to be under the thumb of authority, and trustees wanted as few intrusions as possible into their own expanding, often demanding, lives. Most often, communication regarding the farm was carried out through the informal channels of gossip and the secondhand reports of those living nearby or passing through it. The trustees, now living in such places as California, Ohio, Washington, Iowa, and New York, were also informed by the occasional visits of farmers and former farmers on the road. Some at the farm also maintained or developed direct friendships with one or more of the trustees.

In this way, the farm had proceeded largely unhindered by outside pressure for a surprising quarter of a century. In what amounted to an absence of guiding authority, however, other forms of control had begun to arise.

Those living for long periods of time at the farm, of course, considered it home. This led, as in the case of Janice, to feelings of propriety. While they were not unfounded, these sentiments tended to extend to a sense of ownership as well. The current wisdom at the time of the reunion, though, was that while Janice, Peter, and others had at various times exercised functional control over the farm, they did not ever own it. In later years, both before and after the reunion, several attempts were made to add Janice and others to the board of trustees to give them a larger stake in its ownership, but none of these succeeded.

Those with philosophical or political designs on the farm developed their own forms of influence. Sam, probably the farm's best-known figure, with strong regional roots, saw it as important "liberated territory" and a communal, consensus-run base for political and social change, and he remained closely tied to Janice and the farm, often spending time there, even when he lived elsewhere, and making himself always available for financial, legal, and practical advice, either through his on-the-ground presence or by phone. Through this regimen of personal stewardship and support, he too had developed a serious and widely recognized stake in the identity of the farm.

Harvey held a similar but equally personal vision of the farm. Often over the years, in e-mails, letters, interviews, and conversations, he made a case for it as an important outpost of '60s politics and ideals. In his view, the birth of Montague Farm out of the Liberation News Service bound it, for financial and ideological reasons reflecting its role as a part of the movement, to adhere to the principles on which it had originally been founded and supported. In page after page of intense, passionate argument, and frequent conversations through visits and by phone, he held that as it progressed and aged, the farm was an increasingly rare survival of alternative ideals and practices that needed to be protected and nourished in order to continue to thrive. In Harvey's eyes, the farm was a working commune, a functioning organic farm, a viable ecosystem, a living social experiment, and—equally important on the scale of '60s values he espoused—a fun place to be. That these assertions sometimes shifted, and their ties to important issues and individuals fluctuated, was only one sign of the creative approach Harvey took in what was, in his view, his important role as interpreter of the continuing history of the farm, a role underlined by the regular, if widely spaced, visits he made there.

As the reunion approached, both Sam and Harvey continued their years of work to help define the future of a place they considered, each in his own way, to be essential to their individual vision and—their egalitarian principles notwithstanding—they to it. But in defense of what some saw as a more broad-based set of community values, another form of guidance was explored as well.

Worried by the difficulties of the farm—financial, personal, and organizational, from the mid-1980s through the early 1990s—neighbors, friends, and the extended farm family began to make the case that while the farm might be legally owned by a set of well-meaning trustees, and influenced by strong-willed individuals, its history indicated that its true owners were its stewards—those who ran, looked after, cared about, and paid for it—and that this group, the farm community, deserved a larger place at the proprietary table. The farm had, after all, been founded on a cooperative, communal footing and had increasingly aimed to be part of a larger community of concerned neighbors and friends. In this interpretation, it was the stewardship and principles of shared responsibility characteristic of the history of the farm that ought to take precedence in considering its future. The goal of the community approach to ownership was to keep the farm intact as a good, democratically governed neighbor, a safe locus for social experiment, and a place that might serve others in the future as the flexible way station it had been for so many in the past.

To this end, an informal group began to meet, starting in the summer of 1992, a year before the reunion, to look into issues of governance, organizational models, and the details of the trust. Meetings were held and advice solicited from a local attorney, Tom Lesser, who had always taken an interest in the farm, to clarify the issues involved so that the trust might be modified to benefit the farm and its larger community. Proposals along these lines were then made to the trustees. Though nothing permanent came of them, these proposals and those who devised them provided helpful guidelines and advice for the discussions and decisions that took place during the reunion. Equally important, perhaps, was the clarity that emanated from seeing this strong, community-based effort in action. The farm did have a large family, and that family was legitimately concerned about its life and health. To many at the reunion, looking at the history of the farm and considering its future, a community-based plan best reflected the identity and goals of Montague Farm.

From the meeting notes and communiqués of this self-appointed committee, which came to be called the Friends of Montague Farm, or the Friends for short, the second focus of the general discussion clearly emerges: *How to hold on to the farm.*

One thing nearly everyone in the farm's extended family agreed upon was that if possible the farm should be preserved. Despite its problems, and in spite of its legacy of faction and division, Montague Farm harbored strong memories and important pieces of history and belief for many who had passed through it or were still there. In the minds of most involved in planning for the reunion and thinking out the problems of the farm, its positive contributions and future possibilities far outweighed the difficulties that seemed to plague it. The common assumption in the farm family was that Montague was an important institution under-going adversity and change, and that what it needed was to be turned around and restored to functionality—even advanced into something resembling the formal organization we had once feared—in order to con-tinue its work of social change into the future. Even those who were less sanguine about the farm's future use believed that it should be preserved in some way to honor its notable past and possible potential for good.

Pursuing these two goals led to the other principal issue on the table: *Revising the trust.*

As most in the farm family acknowledged the legal status of the farm and the trust, resolving issues of ownership, preservation, and steward-ship could only be pursued by revising the farm's guiding trust docu-ment. The problems presented by the current situation—distant trust-ees with little involvement in the day-to-day operation of the farm, an ad hoc approach to finances that reflected but did not further a loosely organized commune, uncertain practices regarding residents and their rights—were at least in part the result not only of a laissez-faire approach to interpreting the responsibilities of the trust (the less-is-more, live-and-let-live attitude noted earlier), but also of the broad, uncertain way the trust itself had originally been drawn up. No doubt, like Marshall's will, it was meant to be flexible and open to interpretation. Given the pressures on the farm now, however, as tension mounted and the reunion approached, the quirks and eccentricities of the trust document were found to be as harmful through manipulation as they had been for years helpful in their vagueness and naïveté. To solve the day-to-day problems of the farm, as well as to further its long-term prospects, most of the larger community agreed that the terminology of the trust needed to be sharpened and that some of its provisions required expansion or change.

The Friends

Following initial inquiries to the trustees and conversations with those at the farm beginning in 1991, the meetings of the Friends of Mon-tague Farm were held from the late summer of 1992 well into 1993 and were geared to educating the trustees to the needs of the farm and to supplying the reunion with the necessary grist for its decision-making mill. In a meeting on August 24, 1992, the group produced a draft letter to the trustees. Citing concern about "the long-delayed process of reorganizing the trusteeship of Montague Farm" and the need to address "important issues concerning its future," its "consensus-oriented" view was that if "reorganized in a more democratic and participatory manner," the farm could reach "a fuller potential . . . as a center of agricultural, health, and social/political activity" for years to come.

The draft also reminded the board that on the occasion of the farm's more modest twentieth anniversary in 1988, five years earlier, a large group of its extended family had voted unanimously that several long-term farm residents be added to the trust, and that nothing had been done to complete this. They asked the trustees "to help break this logjam and remove the inertia" plaguing the process of change at the farm and encouraged them, through various suggestions and inducements, to become more actively involved in resolving the current problems at Montague. The "process of broad reorganization" represented in their meetings, they wrote, "will hopefully be concluded by or at the 25th anniversary on August 11, 1993."

By early September 1992, nearly a year before the reunion, the Friends had progressed to a redraft of the Fellowship-trust document, incorporating the suggestions of Tom Lesser. The goals of the changes were:

—expanding the trust;
—encouraging more active "stewardship" of trustees
without individual ownership, liability or inheritance;
—conserving the lands of the farm;
—protecting the farm from sale;
—perpetuating the trust.

The draft, and the group's introductory explanation of it, included numerous suggestions representing the community-centered point of view. It solicited comments from the farm's extended family and asked for other possible nominations to the board. The group's hope was that the proposed changes, backed by the community, would be approved by the board.

At a meeting in late November, the Friends formed committees composed of community members to take on the work it had begun, one for financial planning and management, one for revising the trust, and one to work on planning the reunion. Besides reviewing current problems and possible options for working with the trustees, the group looked ahead to envision life at the farm in a much broader context than had been considered before. The work of the finance and planning committee, for example, was to include exploring such future possibilities for the farm family as health and life insurance, retirement at the farm, investments, and IRAs. The outcome of this meeting was reported to the trustees in mid-January of 1993.

April brought a meeting on legal refinements of the trust; in May, planning began for a financial fact sheet covering the past twenty years of life at the farm. By early July the Friends were writing hopefully, on their own letterhead, to the trustees, outlining the principal goals of the reunion: "healing wounds so that we can culminate the week with an effective revision of the FRY Trust." Several helpful documents were enclosed, with the promise of more to come in the remaining weeks before the reunion.

Susan

Over the course of the meetings of the Friends, Harvey, Sam, Janice, and Peter—as well as many others with long-term interest in or residence at the farm—were all consulted. The efforts of the Friends were meant to be inclusive, and given the thoroughness of their work, the optimism they held for the reunion seemed well founded.

The tone and outlook of the Friends had much to do with farm neighbor Susan Mareneck. One of the good things to come out of the thinking and communication that went into resolving the future of the farm was the emergence in their new adult form of some of the people we had all known there in our twenties. Susan was one of these; Michael Curry, a trustee, would prove to be another. Some of the other trustees distinguished themselves in these discussions as well, along with a few clear voices in the larger community. These participants shared their thoughts and concerns openly and worked to devise new strategies and interpretations that might move what had become a difficult conversation forward toward some reasonable end. Both the individuals themselves and the light they shed provided important guidance throughout the farm's long struggle for definition.

In Susan's case, what emerged over a period of several years was an outlook that combined the taste for independence that had first inclined her to move to the farm and then to become a neighbor nearby, and the quick wit that had seen her through Smith College and a career in the arts and education in New York. Added to this was her leavening experience as a parent and a strongly spiritual element of concern that would eventually lead her to serious involvement with social services and religion.

For Susan, as for some others of the Friends, the practical problems of the farm represented symptoms of something deeper, and to solve them successfully some searching thinking and feeling would be required. Susan had joined the farm a few months after its inception and had become a permanent neighbor only a few months later, when she and her husband had bought the house she had owned ever since. She knew and was for the most part friends with all the principal figures who had moved through the farm over its twenty-five-year life. This provided her with almost an unparalleled view of the farm and its inhabitants over a long period of time. Her perch close to—but not entangled in—its life offered the necessary distance to evaluate it without malice or a private agenda of her own.

But more than that, looking through her letters to those involved, the records from the numerous meetings she organized or conducted, and her own notes as she tried to think through and understand the problems of the farm, the tone that eventually infused the work of the Friends clearly emerges. Susan was interested in straightening out the farm situation. She wanted all those involved to coexist peacefully, to respect each other, to restore the farm to the position of good neighbor and innovative social force it had once held. The route she suggested was cooperation. This would require direct conversations, admissions of fault or misjudgment, possibly mediation. Most important and potentially contentious, it would require each party involved to give up some of what it was contesting. There was no way, she felt, that any one of the parties could truly win without everyone winning something and, in the process, losing something as well.

Susan speaks at the reunion. Photo by Emmanuel Dunand, courtesy FLA.

This was entirely reasonable, and it is one notable aspect of the negotiations over the farm that most of the various positions taken, assertions put forward, and suggestions made were reasonable, at least on their face. Few were outright wrong in the principles they publicly defended or declared during this long process. The problem was more one of mutual accommodation. It was more often the pursuit of particular tactics and strategies in the service of those principles that impeded the progress of the whole.

Susan's contribution to the Friends and the community-based approach to the issues of the farm was the well-grounded social concern and developing humanitarianism she brought to it. In her letters and comments, she repeatedly held out for honesty, directness, compassion, and common sense. Her concern was clearly for the good of the community. Her thoughts were independent and she was one of the few to steer a genuinely neutral course through the choppy waters of the farm debate.

It was really the voice of Susan, along with a few who worked with her—especially Anna and another farm neighbor, Ellen Frank—that stood consistently behind the community approach to the farm's problems. Later, Michael Curry would play a similar role.

CHAPTER 6

Wrapping It Up

The two days of meetings that were the highlight of the farm's reunion followed closely the blueprint provided by the preparatory work of the Friends of Montague Farm. Assembled in a giant, democratically disposed circle in the barn's largest open space, some three stories high and specially cleaned for the occasion, the group conducted its discussions in an orderly, rational manner that only rarely betrayed the strong emotions at play beneath the surface. Following set guidelines, speakers stated their views or rebutted those of others, then passed a symbolic talking stick to the next community member who had requested to speak.

The first round of discussion focused on the qualities of the farm and the reasons it should be preserved. Most were thankful for the maintenance of the farm as "liberated territory," as a center that brought us all together, and as a model for life in harmony with the land. It was pointed out that the farm, for some, was simply home, with all the meanings bound into that freighted term, and that a balance needed to be struck between the lofty goals of the farm and the everyday demands of supporting them.

The next portion of the discussion looked at the legal structure of the farm. Who was ultimately responsible for it? How should they conduct themselves? Here there were many comments on the current trustees, how the trust had been administered up till then, and concomitant suggestions on ways both the individuals and the organization might adapt in the future. Various tasks and responsibilities of trustees were enumerated. Expansion of the board was proposed and a number of new candidates were recorded as offering their services to it.

The following segment of the discussion, often more emotional, was devoted to exploring the problems of the current residents at the farm—particularly some of the budding interpersonal conflicts that had begun to appear.

Last, committees resembling those earlier of the Friends were assembled to pursue what were seen as the principal challenges before the group. One was to look into long-term land use and planning; another was to oversee revising the trust. A third was to deal with finances. A fourth was to focus on communication—newsletters, mailing lists, and

The Big Hug. Photo by Laurie Cohen, courtesy FLA.

the like. Finally, there was a committee made up of farm residents to represent their particular point of view.

Resting after this display of re-creation, all attended a great outdoor dinner in the back yard of the farm. Spirits were high. Sam and Harvey embraced in a show of unity in support of the future of the farm and all it meant. (This gesture, captured on film, was known for years as "The Big Hug.") As afternoon lingered into evening, stories were told, new farmers consorted with veterans of a quarter century before, and there was music and dancing in the barn.

The next afternoon, the new committees reported on their first meetings, setting out business to be pursued in the following weeks and months. Progress had been made. Solid goals had been established for the group to achieve. All looked forward to the projected next annual gathering with the thought that the farm would once again be back on track.

By late November, these deliberations of the demos were translated into a short letter to the trustees, five of whom had attended the event. The letter reported that at the reunion it was unanimously voted that the farm never be sold, and it noted the committees that had been formed to help move farm business forward. The other ten items all related to the trust. They mandated the expansion of the board and named the roughly twenty people willing to serve on it, as well as addressing specifics of committees and voting procedure. The gist of the letter was populist: to set the direction of the trust and the farm in a more consensual, community-oriented direction.

The community, a voice for the idealistic era in which it had been born, had spoken. Board members were asked to sign the letter and return it for the record to the committee charged with revising the trust. At the farm itself, and in outposts across the land, all awaited their response.

7

Aftermath (1994–1999)

The period following the reunion was marked by optimism and a can-do attitude geared toward addressing the goals and actions outlined by the community at its summer meetings. For months, committees continued to convene to develop strategies and refine details for a viable future for the farm. The Land Use Committee searched for relevant documents and approaches. The committee charged with revising the trust explored legal precedents and organizational bylaws that might inform their work. The Finance Committee continued to clarify its analysis of the farm's cash flow and resources. Particular projects took shape: Steve Diamond, a member of the Communications Committee, now back in California, wrote to Susan that he was nearly ecstatic at the prospect of producing a farm newsletter, something he felt sure indicated a new sense of cooperation and collective purpose.

All of this initially boded well for the future of the changes outlined in the summer. As the next few years came and went, though, the efforts first forged by the Friends and then ratified at the reunion again slowed. The agreements outlined in the letter to the trustees were never confirmed. The board, which so many had offered to join, was never expanded. The trust, despite long discussion, remained unchanged. The newsletter, a modest production focusing on the reunion and some interesting facets of farm history, appeared only once.

At the farm itself, life also went on in its essential, querulous, communal fashion, largely as it had before. One change, however, became increasingly noticeable. Over the following few years Tim and Lise, the new tenants brought in by Janice less than a year before the reunion, took on an ever-expanding role. They developed their own approach to filling out the farm, recruiting friends and associates to live at the commune and join in their work. Soon, as Janice had, they thought of themselves as its principal representatives. By late 1994, in an upbeat letter to the farm's trustees and the reunion's Land Use Committee, the undersigned "Montague Farmhouse Residents" reported that they had reroofed the house and added two new dormers. They had also begun reroofing the barn and had repaired windows in the woodshop, cut their firewood for the winter, and finished a new library for the house. Moving on to the main business at hand, the residents proposed constructing a seven-hundred-square-foot maintenance building near the barn for the repair of farm equipment, cars, and trucks. Time was short before winter set in, they said, so it was necessary to clear the site, level it, and bring in twelve yards of stone to prepare for the pouring of the concrete slab that would serve as the foundation for the building. Of the seven who signed the letter, only Tim and Lise had lived at the farm for any length of time before the reunion. Janice was not mentioned at all.

In coming years the Tim-and-Lise family would grow even larger. To Susan and others monitoring the farm in its postreunion state, the chatty, confident tone of their letter—which included plentiful references to compost, haying, organic farming, passive solar heating, and cooperative spirit—with its report of major unilateral improvements and the confident proposal of a building that needed to be started immediately, suggested a precipitous, perhaps even imperious, approach to tending community property. Weren't such things now supposed to be decided by the larger family, and not simply announced to them with little time to effectively respond?

In a letter to the informal group working with her on farm matters, Susan wrote, "There is also the issue of the garage they want to build. . . . Somehow the residents have to realize that it isn't going to work if we are notified at the last moment before they are about to start a significant project, as they did with the roof of the house and now seem to be doing with the garage. We are the closest willing members of the larger family to meet and advise them. . . . There are a significant number of the family who are concerned. We can be the voice of that interest if we are allowed time to express concerns and make the process meaningful."

As time went on, other signs of stress appeared as well. In particular, the relationship between Janice and Lise noticeably deteriorated. Even at the reunion, Lise had already chafed at Janice's continued influence at the farm and offered to take on a stronger role there herself, but the offer had been discouraged as premature by most with longer experience. Now that the community had again repaired to their homes across the nation and the world, she had simply proceeded to advance into that role anyway, broadening her authority and more and more pushing Janice to the sidelines of farm affairs.

Soon Janice was upset enough at the behavior of Lise and her associates to leave the house entirely. In early 1994 she renovated and moved into the old garage, the original Liberation News Service print shop, using the main house only for necessities such as the laundry and the bath. The move was also prompted by the departure of her daughter, Sequoya, the first child to live permanently at the farm. Sequoya had by now graduated from college and was engaged to an international news photographer, reducing Janice's need for room in the house. Her move to the garage followed a two-week trip to France and Spain to visit Sequoya and meet her future in-laws.

A year and a half later, in 1995, Janice left the farm more emphatically to explore living and working opportunities in Colorado; she would return there regularly over the next decade. She locked the door of the garage and did not come back for some time. From Colorado in the summer of 1995, she reported to friends back home that she was happily away from the difficulties of the farm—where, she made it clear, she was often made to feel unwelcome. Although Sam was still in the neighborhood to look out for her interests, this disaffection would continue.

In 1996, Peter Natti, after twenty years at the farm, decamped as well. He had for a long time made regular summer visits to his earlier home in Gloucester, and over the past few years had methodically constructed a woodshop and a small apartment there similar to those he had built at the farm. He undoubtedly had personal reasons for returning to his family home, but to anyone following the travails of the farm in these years, the prolonged abrasive behavior of Tim and Lise and their friends, and ongoing friction with Sam and Janice, seemed an obvious spur to this move. Peter was the last of the farm's longtime residents to leave it, though later, as we will see, Harvey would introduce another view of longevity at the farm.

Generations

The new young generation at the farm was capable; their activities showed that clearly enough. And they were participants in a lifestyle familiar to many in the farm group, as their letter had indicated. They were not, however, great communicators or empathizers. They seemed to lack the humor or social expertise to relate to the larger group—the openness to candid, back-and-forth conversation that occurs among friends—and tended to take refuge, as their occasional bulletins showed, in the more secure generalities of the countercultural life they believed they shared with the farm's extended community.

While many in the farm's larger family were, like Susan, increasingly uncomfortable with this declared but not always welcome association, one important exception steadily emerged. This was Harvey. Even as many others felt a growing distance from the new crew at the farm, Harvey from the beginning had instead found ways to further affiliate himself with them. Sharing their antipathy to Janice and Sam, he found occasions to visit and strengthen his ties with them. When their projects came up, usually a surprise to others, Harvey was often available to support them, even in some cases lending them money to complete them. As the farm's new keepers grew through both fresh recruits and children born or raised there, Harvey, a farm trustee, embraced them as the next generation to carry out the farm's work as he envisioned it.

Thus, an important new dynamic developed in the long-running feud between Harvey and Sam. While for years Sam had been a dominant presence at the farm, in recent times wielding authority through Janice, who still actually lived there, with the advent on the scene of the combative Lise and her coterie, Harvey, from his perch in Ohio, now saw that he, too, could have troops on the ground and compete more effectively in the war for influence over the farm. Indeed, as the conflict continued to develop, this is how the struggle came to be waged.

Consequently, as it turned out, after the apparent success of the reunion, other forces had also been at work. Among the new currents to emerge following the reunion in 1993 was a contentious battle for the legacy of the farm. Though publicly its future was to have been in community hands, privately Sam and Harvey each still harbored the wish to put his own stamp on the farm, and to preserve it in some useful but differing form.

Each in his own way saw the farm as the ongoing embodiment of the idealistic place it had once been. For Sam, this took the shape of supporting those who had themselves actually created the history of the farm and, like himself and a few others, had lived there from its early years. Over the ensuing period, his sympathies and attention would favor the long-term rights of Janice and incline him to lean toward the farm's trustees. For Harvey, the farm's history was best honored through the young people who were living there and using it now and, in his view, enacting in renewed form the farm's original purpose. The result of this discord was a decade of moves and countermoves, legal and ideological maneuvering couched in the terms of a philosophical debate, but leaving the rest of the community alienated and suspicious of the real forces operating behind this long-standing but increasingly desperate battle.

Over this period, Sam and several of his friends turned their attention to the town of Montague and its neighboring villages, where they established themselves, buying houses and entering town government and regional institutions, while Harvey, by various means, worked to cement himself into the current group at the farm, to increase his involvement and stature in national protest organizations, and devise a solution to the farm's problems that did not involve Sam and his circle. As the feud continued, neighbors and friends—some, like myself, from our posts on the fringe—watched the community's consensus-oriented, democratically determined plans unravel, as an immense battle of egos, cloaked in the robes of principle, took shape on center stage.

During these years, with the support of Harvey and the frequent absence of Janice, the new generation of farmers dug in in a serious way.

However tenuous their stature in the larger farm community may have been, alternative careers were pursued, marriages took place, children were born, and the farm remained a counterculture beacon in the area. Although the new farmers used organic methods, they followed a different tack from some of the commune's earlier inhabitants: much of the land they worked was elsewhere, and though apparently scions of a New Age lifestyle, they were clearly achievement-oriented, pursuing their businesses aggressively to support both their outlook and their way of life.

To many, this seemed appropriate. They were, after all, only accomplishing more notably what their predecessors had tried to do with less success: embrace a self-sufficient, sustainable approach to life. This was the side of the new farmers emphasized by Harvey. To their detractors, the new farmers lacked relevant roots at Montague Farm and had none of the broader cultural aims of its original founders. By working elsewhere, they projected something of a carpetbagger image, using the farm as a place to live but evincing none of the magic always thought to surround and enable it.

Of course, given the history of the farm, they did have roots equal to many who had passed through it. Tim and Lise were locals with family only a mile away; Tim had been a schoolmate of Sequoya. They also enjoyed the support of Harvey, a trustee and one of the farm's early members, though often his sentiments were not shared by others.

As their tenure grew, the new farmers, instead, presented a different sort of problem. By accomplishing what others had tried to do—form a family and succeed in supporting it through the local economy—they constituted not a detriment to farm life but an increasingly solid front that alienated Janice and Sam and their circle, who had assumed that through longevity and family ties, the mantle of the farm would continue to lie with them. As Peter Natti pointed out to me, the more solid the new farmers looked, the more threatening they probably became. "All of a sudden there's toddlers back in the farm again," he said, "a new generation coming in, new energy, new blood." Clearly he was suggesting that, in her own eyes, Janice's role had been usurped.

Apart from any personal friction, then, this was a generational change. Indeed, it was literally generational. In the past quarter century, the farm's first child—Sequoya—had grown up and then moved on to begin a life of her own. Now others her age had stepped in. At the same time, in light of this somewhat unwilling transfer, it became clear that over these years the farm, lacking any form of principled renewal other than the thin gruel offered by its current tenants, appeared to many to have exhausted a great deal of its original energy and radical vision.

Could it go further along the original path upheld by Sam and Janice and supported by the large proportion of the farm's family assembled over many years in the crucible of its heated life? Of course. Might it embrace some of the contemporary successors to its important history and turn them to future use, as suggested by Harvey? Certainly. Would it? This was a question yet to be answered.

8

Annus Horribilis (2000)

As the late 1990s unfolded and the millennium neared, the situation at the farm, as it entered its fourth decade, was composed of several related strands. First, the farm was largely controlled physically by its inhabitants, the team of the young organic farmers—Tim and Lise and their friends and associates—who had jelled into what they saw as a new farm family over their more than seven years' tenure there. They were, in turn, supported by Harvey, who continued to offer them both material and moral support and, as a farm founder and a trustee, to champion their cause as embodying the rightful future of Montague Farm.

Then, as the year 2000 approached, Janice, its longest-term resident, made it known that she wanted to return to the farm, abandoning her self-imposed exile after a four-year absence, and that she hoped to move back into the converted garage where she had lived. Just why was not entirely clear. The view she expressed passionately at the time was that the farm was her home and that there was no other place that could satisfy her desire to settle down and continue with her life in the way she chose. Another consideration was the impending birth of her first grandchild—reestablishing at Montague the domestic stability she felt was needed to welcome into the world the next generation of her own family and, as she saw it, the farm's.

Related to these personal motives, especially in view of the way the situation played out, there was also, no doubt, the need for Janice and Sam to reassert themselves at the farm. Janice's departure in 1995 had been preceded by meetings of residents, plus Sam, in which Sam and Janice sought to reexert their authority over the farm. In their view, they wished to return it to a position more closely aligned with the larger farm family and to begin to guide it by a process of decision-making more resembling community consensus. While that approach had had its rough edges—offending, among others, not only Harvey and the current residents but farm stalwart Peter Natti, who at the time still lived there—Janice's intended return to the same situation, which she was discussing in early 2000, had, despite its potential problems, the support of much of the wider farm family and several of the farm's trustees. It was especially supported by Cathy Rogers, who had stayed in touch with Janice over the years, shared her interest in the health field, and sympathized with the domestic concerns she expressed. It was also strongly backed, in recognition of Janice and Sam's role in farm history, by Steve Diamond, who, along with Cathy, represented some of the original voices of the farm. On the other hand, the idea of Janice's return also had the effect of rearousing the enmity of Harvey, who, it appeared to many, had spent considerable effort over the past few years building a bulwark of current residents intended, at least in some part, to block Janice and Sam from meaningful involvement in the farm.

The third important strand composing the farm's situation at the turn of the millennium was that the trust itself, renewed in 1980, was due to expire at the end of the year. At the end of January 2001, unless the board voted to renew it again, the trust would lapse, leaving the seven trustees as merely joint owners of the property—"tenants in common" was the legal term. While under ideal circumstances this transition might have been predicted to occur with little change, as many hoped it would, growing tensions at the farm alerted the board and others in the community to the new possibilities the transition did in fact allow. One of these was that while the terms of the trust made the selling or dividing of the farm very difficult, once it had lapsed any of the seven owners could act on his or her own, creating a situation much more difficult to control. This prospect imposed a deadline of late 2000 or early 2001 for some kind of action concerning the farm and the trust.

Increasingly, the events of the following year would reflect the urgency of this impending date.

As these three themes continued to interweave, others also worked their way into the fabric. Though Janice's concerns were often on the minds of Cathy and other trustees, Susan and the larger community still remained watchful for a solution to the farm's problems that was fair to all. And though the new farm family, as fashioned by Tim and Lise, seemed self-confident in its hold on the land and the place, their sponsor, Harvey, aware of the various pressures now at work, renewed his efforts to explain its presence and shore up its significance. All of this led to what in the end became a monumental effort to finally deal with the long-term issues presented by the farm. How successful this might be, from the vantage point of early 2000, no one knew. By that time, though, one thing was clear: with the stakes high, time short, and tempers increasingly heated, whatever efforts developed were likely to be intense.

Thirty More Years

As the discussion of Janice's return to the farm continued into the new year, and Harvey's effort to oppose it easily kept pace, Cathy asked Harvey directly what objections he had to Janice's plan to move back into the converted garage. Noting that Janice had lived at the farm for some thirty years and already had a widely recognized place there, she admonished him for his often overbearing, self-justifying tone, and in her role as one of the most highly respected representatives of the farm and its life, broached issues that were on the minds of many others. His views were, she pointed out, his own, and not necessarily those of the community he had assigned himself to represent. In positing these views, she continued, he was also asserting a unanimity of group belief belied by the wide variety of people who had passed through and influenced the farm. For someone who believed in consensus, she added, he seemed to have little respect for the views of others.

Leaning, like Susan and the larger community, toward healing and mutual agreement, Cathy suggested a path involving an open comparison of views and the hard work of negotiation. In a position she would keep throughout the year's discussions, she held that if an equitable solution to the problems of the farm could not be found, it would be best for the trust to lapse and for the trustees to deal with the farm simply as owners, unencumbered by all the highly charged issues raised by farm history. Later, in March, she raised the ante further by suggesting that she might cede to Janice her seat on the board, giving Janice a stronger role in determining her own fate and making her an equal to Harvey in the ownership of the farm. Echoing the thoughts of many, she reproached him for holding the farm hostage to his own views.

Coming from Cathy, an influential figure in the farm family, this criticism early in the year affected Harvey strongly. It underlined his isolation from the views of others and initiated a new struggle over definition of the farm and the ideas behind it. Over the next few months, as part of his ongoing contact with many in the farm's extended family, Harvey queried his correspondents regularly about the issues Cathy had raised on which they disagreed. At the end of May, after several drafts and many conversations about them, he addressed these issues in a protracted four-page memo to the community, directed to Cathy. It was titled "30 more years & a new generation." To the extended farm family, the memo had a familiar ring. It was largely filled with positions Harvey had taken for years on the farm, its significance, and its history. But as an explicit, forceful summary of his views offering a sense of the role they would play in the battle for the farm, it makes a good touchstone for the longer debate to follow.

(To remind ourselves again of the farm situation in its larger context, it is useful to remember that Cathy was speaking from Seattle, where she had returned many years before to become a practicing physician. Harvey was an activist based in his native Columbus, writing articles and books on environmental and political issues and frequently venturing forth on speaking tours. Each stayed in touch with friends among the extended farm family, but neither had lived there for many years.)

As an opening gambit, Harvey complimented Cathy on the upcoming birth of her first grandchild, noting that Janice's daughter, Sequoya, was also due. "what could be better?" he asked breezily (in his correspondence, he preferred not to capitalize). He also offered a nod to some recent medical problems she had mentioned: "our hopes are for your mother's speedy recovery." Presumably the inclusive pronoun represented the community he wished to speak for and not the prerogative of royalty it might easily have been taken for.

In his declarations of feelings about the farm, Harvey often spoke of children, families, births, marriages, and other expressions of domesticity. While they may have been employed in part for their salubrious, disarming effect, as the father of five children he could honestly claim a domestic streak of some kind, though to an observer it might have stood somewhat at odds with his frequent travel, demanding work habits, and freewheeling way of life.

Introducing the subject of the farm, he avowed that it remained his "hope and commitment" that "this special place" provide the larger community with another thirty years or more of "shared happiness, productivity and rare magic." Again, these were frequently sounded themes. To Harvey the farm was special and to be viewed as a community resource. Its longevity was significant, its future bright, his commitment to it strong. The phrase "shared happiness, productivity and rare magic" is Harvey's shorthand for his overall view that the farm's countercultural aspect—its role as a hothouse for activism and social change, and as a sanctuary for less conventional modes of life, including the spiritual, superrational, and anti-institutional—was among its strongest traits. That the community should rally to guarantee this role for "another 30 years—at least" was at the core of his hopes for the farm.

Next he suggested that to educate themselves, Cathy and other far-flung trustees of the farm should take the time to visit and to develop closer relationships with its current residents. The farm was strong now, he averred, a tight-knit family well suited to its work on the land and in the community. Without seeing and experiencing the farm and its family, he suggested, it would be difficult to evaluate them and make the decisions about them that the trustees would need to make. He went on to say that he was in touch with the farm monthly and visited yearly, often with his children.

The assertion of the farm's health and the need to become more involved, along with his allusions to domesticity, constituted a central line of Harvey's campaign of persuasion. He noted the generational change that had taken place, allowing this '60s commune to survive as

Harvey walking the walk at the farm, 1969. Photo by Peter Simon, courtesy Beech River Books.

very few others had. In this most recent chapter of the farm's history, he went on, children had been born there and the "hard work and deep commitment" of its current residents, now melded with those of others over the years, had yielded a "human and organic reality" that was both a legacy of our shared past and the key to its future. "without a group commitment," he asserted, "montague farm might well have been lost, to the enormous detriment of the entire community."

Turning to the central component of his argument, Harvey moved from the commitment he had vowed to what lay behind it, again echoing his views over the years. He called this source of motivation "what many of us consider . . . a deeply felt sacred trust," and tied it to an overall "philosophy or vision" of the farm shared by those who had participated in its life—a direct contradiction of Cathy's assertion that the farm had no central overriding tradition to which all adhered.

For Harvey, the trail of this sacred vision or trust led directly back to Marshall Bloom, the farm's founder, his activism, and the important step he took in bringing a group of urban radicals to a piece of neglected rural land in New England. Citing Marshall's work in civil rights, social justice, the founding of the Liberation News Service, and then the back-to-the-land movement, of which the LNS survivors became a part, Harvey saw Marshall's commitments as "pretty clear":

> his principles were of a shared idealism and a higher goal—"liberation"—that meant for at least some of us at the farm an organic sanctuary that was not to be sold or divided, but rather protected and nurtured, in turn to give us amazing opportunities and challenges. to some of us, this has been in essence a spiritual covenant, a spoken consensus, with the force of both the civil law and a higher law.
>
> for some of us, the shared vision has been pretty compelling, and it's been at the core of 30 years of special beauty and communal success.

From this he concluded that the members of the trust Marshall appointed had not been named as "private owners" but as joint "stewards" of this particular vision of the land. In support of this view he quoted from a characteristic, if quirky, document written by Marshall in the early days of the farm. This declaration, meant to express and formalize the nature of common bonds at the farm, spoke of the farm's connection to natural unity and order, and balanced individual independence with the benefits of community interdependence. Importantly, in regard to Harvey, it also bridged the legal and the emotional, noting in its text that such group efforts at public definition were only a necessary measure to protect basic private values, which were finally more important. Naming the farmers "outlaws and renegades"—in the tradition of Pretty Boy Floyd and, more recently, John Wesley Harding—who had banded together "against that which is said to be lawful in the eyes of some," Bloom declared with counterculture gravitas worthy of the Yippies with whom he was then consorting, that "we dismiss the disunity and unnatural world and laws of the society around us with a pick of our nose."

To cement its relevance to farm history, Harvey reminded readers that Marshall's brief tract was read at the twenty-fifth reunion and then printed in the postreunion newsletter. He also noted that in a separate newsletter article Susan had highlighted the community's commitment to the farm and its future, and recounted that they had voted never to sell it. Thus, he wrote,

> there is much . . . throughout the rich and well-documented history of montague farm to say that the "shared vision" and clear consensus among the larger community has been that the farm should not be sold or divided, and should be protected and honored as an organic entity.
>
> and as a result of those commitments, the farm today is solidly poised to survive deep into the next generation, and beyond. it remains a community asset, and a living organic whole. . . .
>
> it reflects a real-world transition for the larger montague community into a sustainable future.
>
> and an extended life for the shared vision that has been—for many of us—at the spiritual core of our individual lives as we have joined around this uniquely powerful farm, which has given us all so much.

He might have added: QED.

Saying he was sorry to have taken so long to answer Cathy's questions—almost four months—he then promised two more memos to further clarify his thoughts.

Harvey's argument about the farm was thus composed of several parts:

—The farm survived today, and its current occupants constituted the legitimate heirs both to the farm itself and to important '60s traditions we all shared.

—The current group had lived there for a significant amount of time, and so deserved the understanding and support of the larger community.

—The birth and raising of their children, their care of the house and land, and other appropriate activities, especially organic farming,

assured the new farm family's right-mindedness, virtue, good intentions, and solidarity with the larger farm community.

The philosophical or "sacred trust" part of his view was based on the
chain of events he had so often alluded to: the lineal descent of the farm
from the Liberation News Service through the benefit film event that
had generated the funds for the "heist" and the move to Montague Farm.
In Harvey's eyes, the farm owed its existence to the movement, to those
who had bought the tickets to the show that had helped pay our way to
the country. To break that chain was to abandon our vows to political
and social change and those who had supported them. In effect, this held
those behind the move, and the trustees who succeeded them, accountable for maintaining a specific mission for the farm. It also devalued the
key revelation expressed by, among others, Steve Diamond in his farm
ur-text *What the Trees Said,* that after the closing of LNS and the beginning of a new era at the farm, we had become "just regular people" living
on the land. (Ray Mungo's first two books, especially *Total Loss Farm,*
had made a similar point.) Further, it marginalized the importance of
Sam and the new activism he had introduced at the farm by lumping all
endeavors at social change there under the single umbrella of heirs to
LNS, in which Sam had played no part.

Harvey's was something of an "originalist," libertarian view honoring the movement "founders" of the farm, a position more familiar on
the right than the left of the political spectrum. It did share with others
in the larger family a belief in the relevance of the past: For a number of
people, in the farm discussion, it seemed that events of twenty or thirty
years ago were still experienced as if they had occurred only yesterday.

From the central role of this sacred trust or shared tradition, Harvey
had concluded that the farm's trustees were not truly its owners but only
its stewards; its owners were the farm community at large, the constitu-
ents of this small democracy. While this did not reflect the details of
the trust, that didn't matter, since the farm and similar anti-institutional
enterprises were beyond mere law, being more an aspect of myth and
renegade society than they were party to the more traditionally organized world around them.

The other two remaining memos he promised ("30 More years, Parts

2 & 3") appeared together as a single message a week later. While reaf-
firming some of the views above it did contain a few new thoughts which
will surface a little farther on.

Reaction

In much of his theorizing, Harvey echoed the views of others in the farm
family. All were glad the farm endured and hoped it would continue; all
supported intelligent stewardship of the land. All respected the farm's
alternative history; all had had some experience with unconventional
interpretations of law and society, even if only through living at the
farm. Most acknowledged some familiarity with spiritual matters; none
believed that the farm should be divided or sold.

The problem with Harvey's views as he presented them was rather, as
Cathy and others had pointed out, that their expression had been carefully tailored to meet his own needs. There was the problem of confla-
tion. Tim and Lise, for example, and the young organic farmers they had
assembled, had indeed established themselves at the farm. Unfortunately,
this did not turn them into natural heirs; Harvey was one of the few who
got along with them. Similarly, his assertion that the term "liberation"
was to be taken to mean "an organic sanctuary" was really no more than
that: his own interpretation of the language. There was also the issue of
language itself. High points in farm and social history tended to be idealized and low ones disparaged; facts tended to be elided. Phrases such as
"many of us," "some of us," and "group commitment," sounded weighty
and important, but often they were transparent stand-ins for Harvey and
his followers. One telling embellishment can be documented statistically.
Harvey's statement that the new farmers had been at the farm for "the
better part of a decade" led him to call their tenure "one third of its life."
They had been there a little over seven years, mathematically less than a
quarter of its history. This may not have sounded quite as persuasive, but
it had the virtue of being true.

The debt to the movement that loomed large in Harvey's view was
also, in the eyes of many in the farm family, open to interpretation. Yes,
a crowd had filled the Fillmore East back in the day to see the American
debut of the Beatles' *Magical Mystery Tour*. In part, this was to benefit

LNS, but in part, of course, it was simply because they wanted to see the film. Certainly there had been an outcry from some quarters when LNS decamped for the country to escape what it saw as its more hard-line colleagues in New York. But the news service had tried to make a go of it for another half a year after its move to the country and failed only in the face of challenges it could never have imagined from the relative cultural security of urban Washington and New York: the demands of rural life away from the support systems and subculture it had depended on. It had, in fact, played a vanguard role in an entirely new front for the counterculture, the back-to-the-land movement. Further, under the tutelage of Sam, the farm had soon reinvented itself as an activist center for another decade before once again momentum slowed. What the farm owed to the earlier movement was not more than it owed its neighbors, friends, and later supporters. There had been far greater public transgressions in the name of the New Age—the alarming exploits of Bhagwan Shree Rajneesh and Jim Jones come to mind. The farm was merely guilty of an open-ended search for itself, certainly one of the sanctioned missions of its time.

The extralegal, mythical spin Harvey put on the farm's history raised a more serious issue. Many of the farm's extended family would agree that "the magic" so highly touted by Steve Diamond, Ray Mungo, Harvey, and others had heavily influenced farm life. What few endorsed was Harvey's harnessing its aura to his own needs.

The conflict alluded to here was whether the farm should be governed by its mythical family—the community touted, if often in actuality disregarded, by Harvey—or its legal owners, the trustees, who bore responsibility for it in the larger, "straight" world beyond its borders. Each of these views held logical and emotional truth. The inability to bridge them in some practical way, or to agree on the nature of the overall, shared vision of the farm, characterized the ongoing discussions about it.

What was the vision of the farm? Many, along with Cathy, would deny a specific institutionalized vision for the farm, but all would agree, she among the foremost, that something resembling a vision, but elusive and less clearly articulated—the then radical, '60s-based, idealistic views leading to so much of the change, risk, invention, and fluidity of the time—was always there just below the surface. This was an important difference. It aligned with the hard/soft, political/cultural distinctions that had earlier troubled the LNS and the Clamshell Alliance. Now these differences had arrived at the doorstep of the farm as well. Typically, the solution to this division had been to go beyond understood norms, to work around agreed-upon rules. There was a history in this group of guerilla approaches to community problems. In this light, Harvey's above-the-law statements were especially significant, portending new encounters to come.

What are the net results of the views revealed in Harvey's memo? A well-buttressed vision not likely to fracture even under the pressure of outside reason or opposing belief; a mix of supporting evidence difficult to separate from its largely internal, personal source, and hard to hold accountable due to its ostensibly reputable roots; small hope of compromise, since communication is difficult when all information is outbound.

The memo and the position it represented set a high bar for discussion. For example, Harvey had expressed the opinion that the other trustees of the farm needed to learn more about its current state, to visit, and to open conversations with its most recent residents. On its face, this seemed a reasonable request. But most of the trustees hadn't lived at the farm for nearly thirty years. They had gone on to pursue their lives, develop careers, take in new directions what they had learned at the farm. To almost all of them, the farm, with its isolated history of fractious contention, now stood apart from the public world in which they lived and worked. From their perches in New York, Los Angeles, and Seattle, they were not likely to suddenly turn from lives and pursuits they had labored to develop to run to the rescue of what they saw as a superannuated social experiment and its heated proponents, to which they now felt connected only through history and personal friends. The request thus ended in an impasse. To Harvey, this proved that his fellow trustees were distant and unresponsive. To others, it suggested different roads to interpretation, such as the one that would later be offered by Michael Curry. For the moment, though, efforts to address the life of the farm would take a new turn.

CHAPTER 8

Tensions Mount

Whatever the strength of Harvey's position, Sam and Janice, for their part, held a similar array of cards in their own hand. While Harvey had been working up his New Age summa over the spring, Janice had been exploring her current options at the farm. As May progressed and Harvey's memo reached its final form, Janice had been privately consulting several in the farm family. Then, under the watchful eye of Sam, she filed a request with the local zoning board to see if the changes she wished to make to the garage would pass muster with the town. This was, as she later explained, a preliminary move meant only to test the waters before making more serious plans to return to the farm. Unfortunately, it also demonstrated not only the limits of Janice and Sam's ability to communicate with the larger farm community but also the general lack of willingness on the various sides of the farm debate to speak openly and share information on the issues at hand.

Hearing of the impending zoning-board meeting only a few hours before it was to convene—through the community grapevine, as often happened in the world of the farms—Harvey, from Columbus, rallied himself and his troops to offer a response. The full complement of current farm residents, including children, turned out at the early-June meeting to request a delay in processing Janice's request. Astonished at the apparent contentiousness on both sides, and not wanting to be caught in the middle, the zoning board readily agreed.

From the point of view of Harvey and the farm residents, Janice's request had not passed through the community channels they now professed to espouse. From the vantage point of Janice and Sam, familiar with the town and its government and with a history of working more closely with the farm's other trustees, this routine step did not seem to warrant the militant response it had elicited. Sam and Janice were angry that her inquiry had been blocked—though legally it had merely been tabled or delayed. Each side faulted the other for lack of communication.

To others, this skirmish appeared to have an obvious trajectory. Janice, with the allied expertise of Sam, had attempted to work around the farmers; the farmers, with the assistance of Harvey, had rallied to protect what they increasingly saw as their own turf. All of this was additionally confusing, since only a day or two before the community had received a long and cordial newsletter from the residents of the farm, and Harvey's "Parts 2 & 3" memo had surprisingly offered major concessions to Janice. The only reasonable explanation was that the two opposing sides were not talking, and that their planned actions were entirely uncoordinated, passing each other, so to speak, as ships in the night. Where these vessels touched in passage, however, sparks flew.

The evident friction and the public nature of this display caught the farm's larger community by surprise, spurring a number of responses. Theorizing about the farm's current and future state increased dramatically. Innovative solutions promoting discussion and change were proposed. With the extended family now alerted to a new level of hostility, the tenor of the conversation became more serious and a long season of work on the farm's problems began. As John Wilton wrote to his fellow trustees in the wake of these events, and with the approaching end date of the trust in mind, "We have until February to avert a train wreck."

Among the trustees, it was John who, with this deadline looming, was first motivated to set to work to find a comprehensive solution to the farm's problems before the board should be overtaken by them. Michael, also a trustee, commenced what became a rigorous process of rethinking the philosophy behind the farm and the trust. In the larger community, Susan proposed assembling a working committee, along the lines of her earlier Friends group, to form a new, nonpartisan trust to buy and oversee the farm. A farm neighbor suggested a course of mediation, and from the far West, the generous and spiritually oriented Steve Diamond, a trustee as well, either from desperation or inspiration, proposed simply giving the farm away to the Peace Pagoda, a local Buddhist organization.

During this period, other developments surfaced that would remain part of the farm dialogue. Lazarus, actually named James Tapley or Jamie, not heard from for twenty years and believed by many in the farm family to be dead, once again lived up to his name by suddenly reappearing, against all expectations, to take an active part in the discussion. Over the intervening years he had become a master bookbinder and an expert on Islamic art, and he was again living in his native Florida. This seventh trustee, his opinions, his working methods, and his vote would prove influential. The new view of farm philosophy jelling from the reflective deliberations of Michael Curry, now a professor of geography, would also offer a novel and significant perspective. As the trustees wrestled with the ultimate fate of the farm, two further issues of importance resurfaced as well: whether the farm could be divided or sold, and if so, whether anyone should be allowed to profit from it. These were of concern to both Harvey and the farm residents, and to Susan and her new committee, none of whom believed that either should occur. They were certainly of interest to the trustees, who, as owners, were those who might actually benefit.

In light of these mounting considerations, John set off in late July to spend two weeks in and around the farm to see what could be done to repair the situation, bring the sides of the dispute together, and launch the farm on a new era of cooperation. He returned to New York with some ideas and the outline of a plan.

This was a period of ferment in which various options were proposed and discussed. As August dawned, the trustees, led by John and Michael, were working toward what appeared to be a viable solution honoring most of the factions involved. At this time, it took the form of a four-point plan, one of many that would be discussed: the farm's wild land would be protected in conservation; the garage would be given to Janice; the farm, minus these two elements, would be offered to its current inhabitants at some fraction of its market value when it was established; the trust would be dissolved. There were still some sticking points, but as this plan, at the time called "the peace plan," seemed to resolve the most contentious issues, the mood in the family at this point could be characterized as cautiously hopeful.

Shortly after John returned home, however, came the second unexpected blow of the summer. During the time he had been visiting, negotiating, and speaking openly with the current farmers, Harvey had been directing them privately along a different track. In early August, it was discovered that, together, Harvey and the farmers had formed a new organization of their own, the Montague Evergreen Foundation (MEF). In a brief legal document called a quitclaim, filed in late June, Harvey had given over his place on the original trust to the new foundation, putting a public face on his belief that the farm community, as he saw it constituted, should own the farm, and that he eschewed any personal benefit from its changing hands, if that were to occur. Now, apparently, it was Harvey's turn to be angry.

The problems raised by the quitclaim and the Montague Evergreen Foundation brought the whole matter of the farm and the trust to a new level of confusion and consternation. Thenceforth, Harvey presented himself, when needed, as only one of the voting members of this new organization of which little was known. When necessary, though, he also participated in discussions of the original trust, though in theory he had given his seat on it away. But a reading of the trust showed clearly that board members were not allowed to unilaterally transfer their interest in the trust; in other words, that the quitclaim was probably not legal. That didn't seem to affect Harvey, who was also on record as believing in the validity of the reconfigured board envisioned at the reunion in 1993, making him a member of three competing boards at once. Intoxicated with the mythical importance of his actions, he appeared little concerned with their strict legal interpretation. Finding the philosophical elements of his lengthy memos to have been unconvincing, he had turned to more practical means.

There were also personal and moral issues to be addressed. How, John fumed, could the farmers they were trying to help, and his old friend Harvey into the bargain, have pretended to be negotiating with him face to face while behind his back arranging to oppose him? And, echoed others among the trustees and the farm community, how could such people ever be trusted again?

The most serious consequence of the quitclaim and the arrival on the scene of MEF was not merely anger, but that it brought yet another entity to the table. Whether or not the new organization had any existence other than on paper, or Harvey's attempt to give over to it his interest in the original trust had any legal validity, the filing of papers assured that the interests of the current farm residents—whichever of them suited Harvey's needs—would have to be considered as the discussion progressed. This had the effect of prolonging and complicating the process of resolving the issues surrounding the farm, while the goal of the majority group of trustees and the larger community was to wrap it up.

Shortly after the discovery of the quitclaim and the MEF, Susan's new working committee presented its first proposal to the larger community. Entirely reasonable and the result of much work, it suffered from the repercussions of the heated activity surrounding it. The main points of this proposal were the formation of a new trust, the sale of the farm to the new trust at two-thirds of its value, when appraised; the division of the proceeds between the present trustees—who were beginning to take a financial interest in the transaction—and the new trust which would administer the farm, and the setting aside for Janice of either a small parcel on which to build (though she wouldn't own it) or a sum of money. The costs of these arrangements were to be covered by a new mortgage; the old one had been retired in 1993, one of the reasons the farm had become such a focus of interest: it was now debt-free. Mortgage payments would be made by residents of the farm along with the trustees, who would be asked to contribute an annual membership fee. Outside fundraising was also considered by the working committee to be a feasible way to generate income for the farm.

By this time the conversation had reached a higher pitch, and expectations on all sides had formed more clearly—though unfortunately not in agreement with one another. To Susan and her group, the proposal represented a fair deal for everyone, with compromise on all sides. To the trustees, this altruistic view did not reflect the financial realities that were emerging concerning the value of the farm. They also mistrusted the committee itself because it included residents of the farm, though a close look would have shown that they were included only among a set of varied members of the larger community. As Laz wrote to Susan a few days after the proposal had been presented, when all arrangements were completed the new trust would be buying the farm for less than a third of its market value, and the trustees would receive only a fraction of what they were coming to feel was a fair recompense for surrendering their interest in a valuable property. He pointed out that, legally, it was the duty of each trustee to obtain the maximum benefit for the entire trust, and that they could be sued if they did not. In other words, that any plan that could not garner the entire seven votes of the trust was not worth discussing. Considering the recent behavior of Harvey and the current farmers, Laz added, he and other fellow trustees felt no need to subsidize their way of life by offering them the farm at a reduced cost.

As a result of the turmoil surrounding this roughly two months' activity, its tone changed again. John, Michael, and Laz, who had been exchanging opinions only informally, began to see the need to work together and started speaking to one another in greater earnest. After the legal shocks of the zoning-board debacle, the quitclaim, and the new MEF, they also reluctantly initiated consultations with an attorney. Eventually Cathy and Steve Diamond joined them as well. In addition, the financial value of the farm having come increasingly to the fore, discussions of that aspect of the matter became lengthy and complex, eventually settling into a more regular pattern as accurate information about it became available. Finally, Steve Marsden, the trustee least heard from after the rearrival of Lazarus, began to weigh in. His opinions, quite different from those of the others, like those of Laz, would, to their surprise, come to affect them as well.

Michael's View

Out of all the ferment over the farm, some good things did eventually emerge. As seen earlier, there were the efforts of Susan and her groups, as well as the concerned action of the larger community surrounding the farm and its life. There was the reappearance of Lazarus, lost to most in the community for some twenty years. There was the salutary example of the trustees working together using the best of their abilities and getting to know each other probably better than they ever had before. Even on the negative side of the scale, the ongoing battle between some of the principals in the fight for the farm revealed important lessons about people and their motives, even if we would have preferred not to know about them.

One of the best of these developments was the thought put into the history and significance of the farm by Michael Curry. As each in the battle for the farm rallied to do his or her best to advance their views, personalities and traits were revealed that might otherwise have remained hidden in the relative obscurity of private lives. John, first to jump in on the side of the trustees, proved adept at the diplomacy and strategy one might have expected from his wide-ranging, well-educated background. He was also a good judge of character, and often took a broader, historic view of farm events, as befitted one conversant in equal measure with the classics and the news. Added to these, he had an acerbic way with language that leavened with much-needed humor his disgust at the behavior of some involved. Steve Diamond, as always, proved more spiritually oriented and idealistic, often entering the discussion from difficult-to-track corners of consciousness that led John to worry occasionally about Steve's habit of, as he put it, "leaving the reservation." Lazarus revealed how much the no-nonsense side of him, prominent even in the late '60s, had grown since we knew him. Cathy, our former "earth mother" (today she would probably be amused by the term), remained the most emotionally anchored of this group, which made up the majority of the trustees.

The contribution of Michael, at this time approaching the midpoint in a twenty-five-year career as a professor at UCLA, also reflected his abilities and beliefs, and went a long way toward clarifying thinking about the meaning of the farm and our experiences there. Beginning in May of this year, 2000, as he watched the situation of the farm escalate, talked it over with others, and reviewed Harvey's drafts for his lengthy memo, he, like John, was motivated to take a more thorough look at the underpinnings and implications of the discussion. Over the summer his thoughts developed into a distinct interpretation of his own.

In mid-May he wrote to Harvey, reviewing the current situation, making some suggestions and offering an eight-point plan for the farm. A notable part of this plan, besides the matters of ownership, value, and rights common to most of the plans put forth, was his suggestion to give any proceeds of a sale of the farm to a nonprofit organization or "some other sort of socially/politically useful memorial." That is, that no individuals would benefit from it and that any profits would go to something that "allows us to acknowledge the fact that we all agree after all of these years on a great many things—the importance of the environment, social justice, cooperation, and working things out." This potential link between past, present, and future became the backbone of a larger theory.

Indeed, he wrote, despite the evident strengths of the farm—its buildings and land, its organic farming, its role for some as a way station in life, "I think that it might be useful to begin to ask what we think makes the place important":

Michael Curry, Vermont, 2011. Photo by author.

> Certainly for me, and for a long time, it was a kind of symbol of the hope for a better world. And for a long time it seemed to me that the fact that the place was there attested in some way to that possibility.
>
> I no longer think that. In the last years, and certainly since the 25th reunion, it has seemed to me that the place has come to symbolize something else—the intractability of people's positions, the inability to change . . .

Like others of the earlier era that had spawned the farm, now in their fifties, Michael was reconsidering his experiences and beliefs. As John would later put it, a number of the trustees felt that the adventurous, pioneering, socially significant role of the farm as a physical place had long since dissipated.

A week later, ruminating with John on steps to be taken in advancing the farm conversation, he considered the principal difficulty attached to giving Janice a place at Montague—that it involved dividing the farm, something no one really wanted. This recalled to him a passage in a book he had read about Black Mountain College, a progressive, experimental liberal arts school that survived less than twenty-five years after its founding in 1933. Besides his ties to the farm, Michael had also been involved in the tumultuous life of a small midwestern college that had had many of the same sorts of problems, so the passage had particular resonance:

> I too had a hard time with the idea of splitting the land. I was reminded, though, of once reading Martin Duberman's great book on Black Mountain College. The college had gone through many of the travails of the farm. One day a couple of people—maybe Charles Olson, I can't remember—met in a cafe and said, "OK, let's just shut it down; Black Mountain can continue in spirit elsewhere—and everywhere."
>
> When I first read that many years ago it was like being kicked in the stomach; I couldn't believe that they would do it. But over the last year or so what they did has come to me to make a lot more sense.
>
> In fact, it seems to me that now the spirit of Montague exists almost everywhere but at Montague. It certainly is alive and well when you and Steve and Cathy and I talk about the place and the people, and worry about how to make things work. So perhaps, as in the case of Black Mountain, it's time to close off this part of the story.

This set of thoughts capsulized Michael's developing view that the life of even a successful, altruistic organization can flag, but, importantly, that its spirit can move on.

Five days later, toward the end of June, in a note to the other trustees, he outlined and commented on some of the issues then on the table— a conservation easement, dividing the land, selling the buildings and remaining land to the current residents, and, again, donating the proceeds of any sale to a nonprofit group. This latter point led him into a new area: their own lives. Harking back to his insight about Black Mountain College, he wrote:

> A final comment: Thirty years down the road almost all of us have

spent almost all of that thirty years physically far from Montague. But in an increasingly greedy and individualistic world, each of us still spends his or her time in pursuits not that different from those in which we were engaged thirty years ago. Politics, environmentalism, healing, teaching, music, writing. These are all pursuits that aim to make the lives of others better, and not just to increase our personal wealth or power.

And it seems to me fitting that we close off this phase of our lives, where the farm was a real physical place, and move to one in which it is simply an idea, with this last gesture of generosity—to the land, to Janice, and to others engaged in the causes in which we believe.

The next day, he took this a bit further. In response to a comment from John, he admitted: "Well, I guess you ferreted out the central inconsistency in my proposal. On the one hand, I say that we are all doing valuable stuff. On the other, I suggest that we give proceeds of a sale to other groups so that they can do valuable stuff."

He amended his proposal to bring the donations and the lives together by offering part of the proceeds of the farm, if sold, to each of the trustees, in order to help them continue with the socially, culturally, and politically engaged lives he had described. This and some other arrangements he suggested would also help bridge the gap between those who thought that no individuals should benefit financially from the farm, and the new notion that whatever the farm itself contributed to social change was no more important than that contributed by other members of its community.

By late September, reviewing the many months, even years, of conversation and controversy, and considering their sources in the history of the farm, Michael arrived at the conclusion, which he set out in a three-part draft to John, that the farm battles were being fought on the wrong ground.

In the first section, "The Farm and the Fellowship," he contested the notion that the legacy of the farm revolved about its land. Marshall's will, he pointed out, focused on maintaining the "fellowship" he had created, the FRY, which later became the trust. The will did not even mention the farm. "My reading is this: The will involved Marshall's creation of a group, the 'Fellowship of Religious Youth,' and it involved his implicit charge to that group to carry on in a way consistent with his political and cultural views. The farm was incidental to that charge." Indeed, he pointed out, Marshall had lived on the farm for only about sixteen months, and some members of the trust far less. "I would argue that he picked the seven of us because he had an intuition that we would in some way—and in contradistinction to the others living at the farm at the time—carry on in a way with which he would feel comfortable."

From here, Michael incorporated his idea of the lives of these trustees—Harvey as environmental activist; Cathy as healer; the Steves, Marsden and Diamond, devoted to the peace movement; Lazarus's work with books and Islamic art; John's with Indian music; and his own with teaching. These were the sorts of work, he suggested, of which Marshall would have approved; some thirty years later, he would not likely have been found still living on an organic farm. The implication was that the attention on the farm itself was misplaced: "Indeed, to focus on the farm is to suggest that Marshall was just completely wrong, simply because every single one of us has left it. . . . Rather, it seems to me that Marshall had a clear vision, that of those living at the farm, seven of us had the wherewithal to move on, to address the world as it changed, and to try to save what is good in that world and change what is not." In this way, he aligned a new concept of the fellowship with the earlier outlook of the farm.

In the second part, "The Fellowship and the Trust," Michael pursued his assertion that "our focus needs to be on the Fellowship and the Trust, and not the farm; it needs to be on what one might take as a covenant that Marshall attempted to create, a pact with each of us, charging us to act in a particular way: "Marshall, simply put, made a judgment about people, about their political views, but also about whether they belonged together, whether one could reasonably see them as potentially having some long-term connection with one another."

Using this standard, he named eight others who might well be considered part of the Fellowship, and, he suggested, there were probably more. "Each of these people has in some way been an essential part of the project of the Fellowship, and most listed here have shown that by their involvement in the attempt to resolve the issues raised by the upcoming expiration of the Trust as a legal entity."

John Wilton (*left*) being presented with the Jyotsna Award at the 8th Annual
Chhandayan All Night Concert of Indian Classical Music, Cathedral of St. John the
Divine, New York, 2006. Photograph © 2006 Jack Vartoogian/FrontRowPhotos.
All rights reserved.

What is particularly surprising is that this was not the list many
would have expected. Sam and Janice, for example, on one side, were not
on the list, nor on the other were the current farmers. But this, he went
on to say, was the problem:

> I recognize that this may be a controversial list. There is certainly
> room for argument, for an addition here and a deletion there. More
> controversial, though, may be the fact that this list excludes some
> people who are widely viewed as having been closely connected
> with the farm. But I repeat: a connection to the farm is not the same
> as a connection to the Fellowship or the Trust. And I would sug-
> gest that in various ways those others have demonstrated that they
> lack in some fundamental way those elements that were meant to
> be at the core of the Fellowship, and that are thereby requirements
> for addition as members of the Trust.

We have seen this when various individuals worked to force others out, or treated the place as a kind of boarding house, or attempted to take possession of it for themselves. Those who have engaged in those actions may have lived on the farm, but they have not demonstrated that they are part of the Fellowship.

The third section, "Whither the Farm," underlines his belief that the original intent of its founder was that the Fellowship, and later the trust, take a guiding role in the farm and its life: "From my perspective, if we look at matters in this way, and look at the current status of the farm, one thing is certain. Given what we have learned about the current residents of the farm, both by looking at what they do and by attempting to negotiate with them, they are not the sort of people whom Marshall would have included in the Fellowship."

Thus, he says, the trustees have no responsibility to them, and certainly none to subsidize their lifestyle by giving them an easy deal on the farm. "In terms of meeting the aims of the Fellowship," he concludes, returning to his earlier analysis, "a far better way is to subsidize the work of the original members."

Like Harvey's lengthy memo, this elaboration of Michael's thoughts can serve as a useful reference point. Others on the board and in the community responded very favorably to the interpretation he was developing and his comments on farm life. They seemed to touch on something important that all understood, and to weigh the dry, humorless, self-interested discussion that had gone before against the vibrant spirit many had felt at different, more substantially engaged periods in the life of the farm.

Cathy was said to have been prompted by Michael's thoughts to contrast the depressing farm debate with the freshness of waking by the ocean at her newly opened health spa, a conceit that brought home the difference between the tenacious adherence to a dubious set of self-serving "principles" that seemed to guide the farm-based side of the debate and the new, more fully grounded lives of the larger community and most of the trustees. Irv, now an attorney in New Jersey, wrote on the day he set aside each year to remember the death of Marshall that he thought that there was indeed a fellowship. "Those ties . . . are not material links," he wrote. "While everyone might not line up behind Steve

Diamond's Peace Pagoda, I think it's closer to where the farm should be going. That is, to maintain it as a community institution."

Steve Diamond himself later wrote to Michael, "my belief has been what you expressed . . . that the f. r. y . went out into the world, and thus our locus has become everywhere, by common agreement." Chuck Light at Green Mountain Post Films, who followed farm affairs closely, later wrote that most of the trustees had stayed in touch with the extended farm family, and had often worked together with them on projects as part of "what I would term a greater fellowship."

In light of the ongoing acrimonious debate, Michael's memo received an overwhelmingly positive response. To his original thoughts he eventually added a few related observations: that under current plans, the mortgage payment for the farm, shared by its seven residents, would be less than the common cost for a one-bedroom apartment; that his wife's and daughter's work for social change in Europe and California seemed a clearer expression of the idealism of the farm's founding than the attitude of its current residents; that his own efforts to promote a useful harmony in the charged setting of academic departments and committees made it clear to him that in the farm situation, as in most others, compromise was going to be necessary on all sides. Such translations from the life experience those of our age now all shared, portrayed contentious issues in usefully familiar terms, and served to separate the well-reasoned portion of the discussion from that which was largely opportunistic or doctrinal.

Debating the Farm

By now, some eight months into the year, and with five months remaining until the trust would lapse, the sides had become fairly clearly defined. The five majority trustees—John, Michael, Laz, Cathy, Steve Diamond— were motivated by the ideas embraced in the Fellowship outlined by Michael and were concerned with the legal and financial implications stemming from their ownership of the farm. Harvey and the current farm residents adhered to his own views, especially that the farm should not be sold, and that even if it were, no individuals should profit. The seventh trustee, Steve Marsden, in left field both ideologically and geographically from his bicoastal colleagues, wrote occasionally from Iowa.

His view focused on a very rigid reading of the trust document that was in a sphere of its own. His opinions, though personal and of a different nature, aligned in practical ways with Harvey's in his adamant agreement that the farm should not be divided, sold, or turned to profit. The community, represented by Susan and her group, stood for informed discussion, mediation, compromise, and a fair deal for all sides. Janice and Sam still held out for her place at the farm and for their restored influence there. Others weighed in from the fringes of the debate when they could make themselves heard.

One of the problems with this diverse array of players was that each tended to move at its own speed and in its own sphere. As in the cases of the zoning-board incident and then the working-committee proposal, letters or messages would be sent or calls made, proposals circulated, actions proposed, or strategies developed largely in isolation. As a result, the working committee, for example, continued to propound an idealistic view of the farm and its future while the trustees had already come to the conclusion that such an outlook was impractical and anachronistic. Similarly, the current residents continued to view themselves as the natural inheritors of the farm, when most around them did not, and long-term strategies were worked out by differing groups whose guiding principles were never likely to be brought into agreement.

Ironically, at various points in this long process, as some were able to see, the different sides were not very far apart. Unfortunately, the accumulated animosity and dysfunctionality evident among them kept them from developing any useful process for solving their problems together.

In this atmosphere of uncoordinated controversy, events continued into the fall. In late August of 2000 several key figures held a meeting at the farm that seemed to bode well for a collective solution. This eponymous "meeting on the hill," chaired by neutral observer and farm friend Dan Keller, offered concessions to all sides and was briefly thought to be the beginning of a solution. It was later rejected by the residents of the farm, who had earlier approved it.

In late September, an appraisal of the farm was completed. Its estimated market value of some $345,000 was far above what most had

expected. This complicated negotiations on several scores. For the trustees, it reinforced the view that the farm couldn't be given away for too
little, since their legal duty was to do the best they could for the trust as
a whole. For the working committee, it raised the bar, since if a new community-based trust were to buy the farm, they would be paying a great
deal more for it. For Janice and Sam, it stretched whatever resources they
were planning to assemble should the chance arise to reclaim or buy the
farm. To those dug in, Harvey and his group, it served to increase the
value of what they were already fighting for.

The appraisal helped stabilize the trustees' financial thinking. From
this point on, the "bottom line"—or "payout," as the peremptory Laz
had come to call it—that had begun to figure strongly in their thinking
could be better calculated, finally resting, after the other considerations,
in the range of $20,000 to $40,000 per person—$15,000 to $50,000 at
its extremes. Such personal gain was, of course, anathema to others in a
farm family attuned to the good of the community. But the crux of the
matter was this: If the various factions of the farm's family could not
agree on how it was to proceed into the future, and seemed able to rally
only on the field of battle, what good lay in simply maintaining the farm
and renewing the trust? Wouldn't the current well-established impasse
just continue? Even if a renewed trust and all the liabilities that accompanied it were taken on, wouldn't the two major combatants—Harvey
and Sam—just continue to fight it out as they had for years, to the ongoing detriment of the rest of the community?

This was certainly the view of the five majority trustees. As they saw
it, the farm had to be sold, one way or another, whether to an individual
or a group, in order to clear what John called the "horrific karma" that
had developed there over the preceding years. It could of course be given
away, but to whom? As Laz had pointed out, it would have to be given
to someone on whom all agreed, and consensus didn't appear to be lurk-
ing anywhere nearby. It had to be sold because the community could not
arrive at a peaceful, workable, cooperative solution to its problems. Viable
solutions proposed at large were not agreeable enough to the warring
parties to carry them; those imposed unilaterally by each of the factions
only drove them farther apart.

Of course, once the idea of selling the farm arose, it took on a life of its own. Though the trustees backed into it, and would certainly have simply renewed the trust if it had been feasible, the influence of money eventually cast its well-known spell. In the presence of the farm, its land, its buildings, and its history, or in conversation with those who valued it, it was difficult to imagine taking on responsibility for its dissolution, or really its diminishment in any way. With the growing realization of the stalemate there, however, and the probable impossibility of a solution amenable to all, the idea of a payment to each of the trustees in return for cutting the farm's karmic Gordian knot became far more attractive. Thus, unappealing ideas become less so and untenable ideals translate into viable if not agreeable action, as Michael had pointed out.

A month after the appraisal, the working committee submitted its second, revised proposal to the trustees and the larger farm family. Its principal goal was to continue the farm as a social experiment under community control and to preserve it from outside sale. The specifics of the proposal attempted to make its overall, community-oriented view more appealing to all sides. For the trustees, though, the $150,000 it offered them did not meet the figures they had been discussing among themselves. The net result of the committee's proposal was, then, perhaps more damaging than helpful to its cause. As one of the trustees wrote to the others, "Amazingly, told that their offer was too low, they made an even lower one!" Though the community continued to defend and explain it, the proposal never gained the traction it needed to become a workable plan.

One troubling aspect of this part of the discussion was that a vocal portion of the farm's extended community continued to believe that it was not truly owned by the trustees at all. As one longtime resident wrote in support of the working committee's new proposal, "The farm was never 'private property.'" Such views in the farm community rightly reflected the mythical side of its history. Unfortunately, they also served to underline the trustees' opinion that those with whom they were speaking about the farm held only idealized, unrealistic views about it and thus that they were, in the long run, better off simply dealing with it among themselves.

At this point, after some four months spent watching John's struggle to negotiate a workable plan for the farm, Laz, who always espoused a quick-moving approach, began to press ahead. Graciously thanking John for his work, which he truly appreciated, Laz in late October called for a plan from Sam and Janice, to see whether they were prepared to buy the farm themselves. Sam had been closer all along to the trustee majority and had a reputation for negotiation and practical solutions. While Harvey had sought influence over the farm from afar, Sam had always taken an on-the-ground approach, assisting, cajoling, motivating, and saving it personally at various times, when needed. Also unlike Harvey, he had maintained his friendships among the majority of the board who, while wary of him because of the self-interest of his position on the farm and the leverage he sometimes applied through his knowledge of the law, still favored him over his sometimes less nimble but often equally powerful counterpart in Columbus.

(Notably, Sam had studied the law and theories of social justice intensely in order to defend himself at his 1974 trial and later became a lawyer himself. Harvey, a trained historian and an activist, had for years also focused on issues of social justice. He was not an attorney but, relevant to the farm story, he had married one. As in other ways, in these ways, too, these two opponents were functional equals.)

The closer involvement of Sam and Janice first took the form of a five-page plan from Sam in early November that included adding Sam, Janice, and Dan to the trust and taking out a mortgage to help pay for the farm. By adding to the board, the five trustees working together would then have the majority needed to override dissident members Harvey and Steve Marsden on important issues. They would also, however, as some of them pointed out, be opening themselves up to further manipulation by Sam and Janice, which, owing to their new status, would now be more difficult to control. Eventually, this plan evolved into adding only Janice to the board. Papers were drawn up to hold an election, and voting by the trustees on the addition of Janice to the trust began in late November.

Thus, as December 2000 opened, the trustees were considering Sam's plan and voting on adding Janice to the board. They also continued to consider the working committee plan. John was keeping their attorneys up to date on the trustees' thinking and on the several options now on

Cathy and Laz at the farm, 1970. Photo by Christopher E. Green, courtesy Beech River Books.

the table. Other currents on the trustees' side included seconding Sam and Janice's desire to evict the farm's present tenants at the earliest possible date, and continuing actual skirmishes with them—Lise, at the farm, had instructed some involved in the negotiations not to speak to anyone. There were also many comments from the larger farm family expressing concern and amazement at the pass things had come to at Montague Farm.

Into this latter category fell a long letter from Marty Jezer of Packer Corners, Montague's sister farm half an hour away. Marty was a long-time activist and writer with a strong concern for social justice. He had worked with both Sam and Harvey and was a friend or colleague to many in the extended farm family and in the regional community. He wrote to endorse the working committee's plan and to support the rights of those currently living at the farm, though he was not personally close to them. His opinions are of interest because they point up another complicating strand in the larger discussion. Those who were most familiar with the farm in its current form through living in the neighborhood or region, or who shared its circumstances—like Marty, living on a similar farm— tended to view the situation quite differently from those who, as Michael had pointed out, had left the fold to go on to other things. The view of the farm from a more distant perspective was that it was dysfunctional; as John had said at one point, "We believe that Montague Farm as a worthwhile institution has long since played itself out." The view of close neighbors tended to be more personal, and many of them saw the farm as, if troubled, still functioning and worth saving. Such a difference among people of otherwise similar generational and philosophical outlook unfortunately helped amplify some of the ongoing rifts in the discussion.

The Complaint

As the end of December neared and the holidays loomed, with a little more than one month to go before the lapsing of the trust, the third of the blows administered by Harvey that year was delivered. In a registered letter to all the farm's trustees and Sam and Janice, the new Montague Evergreen Foundation announced that to clarify the title of the farm they had sought the help of "an independent third party." While the letter encouraged mediation and negotiation, its main import was very clear: They intended to go to court.

Though the trustees didn't see them for some time, the papers on which this letter was based, a "complaint" of some ten pages, had been filed three weeks earlier. This document, familiar from the obvious presence of Harvey's rhetoric and point of view, also contained some interesting new strategic turns. Principal among them was that Harvey, according to the legal reasoning that follows, was himself the only true owner of the farm, and thus that its title ought to revert directly to him. He would then convey it to the new Montague Evergreen Foundation. The reasoning was that at the time of the renewal of the trust in 1980, Harvey was the only one of the original seven trustees still living at the farm. Since, the complaint asserted, the trust documents stipulated that trustees forfeited their role if they left the farm and the Fellowship, Harvey, being the last man standing, had actually unknowingly owned the farm for the preceding twenty years!

The complaint's thirty-seven points were preceded by an introduction "for information purposes only" outlining Harvey's now exceedingly familiar views, from the benefit Beatles showing to the status of the current farmers, his high school acquaintance with Marshall, and the "original mandate" that the farm be "a non-profit organization, serving the higher goals of peace, human harmony and organic living." The legal links appear fairly thin: A lengthy footnote explains how he happened to overlook his new status for twenty years. The moral links, as those commenting on it later pointed out, bordered on the absurd. Contravening the intentions of the larger community, refusing meaningful negotiation, and suing the widely acknowledged legal owners of the farm didn't seem the best way one might have chosen to serve the higher goals of peace and human harmony.

The introduction was important, though, since without its supporting claims the complaints made by the MEF would have had little context or meaning. The case made by the complaint was that Harvey was the true owner of the farm, and that due to actions of the trustees and their compatriots (or, in the case of Sam, merely by implication), title to the farm had been clouded. The trustees' principal error, the document alleged, had been not renewing the trust on the exact date of its expiration. (It had not been filed until several years later.) Janice's offense had been to "seize and occupy" the garage in 1994 and then recently to plan to expand it. Both Sam and Janice were alleged to have unlawfully claimed the rights of owners and trustees. Besides the usual court costs and such "other and further relief" deemed just by the court, the remedies sought included the repossession of the garage from Janice; that the court rule that the farm could not be divided; that it rule to clarify the title to the farm—presumably in favor of MEF, to whom it had theoretically been conveyed by Harvey; and that the current residents be granted the status of life tenancy at the farm.

Practically, the complaint set legal wheels in motion that had to be addressed. Strategically, though, it appeared to be only the latest chapter in what was now coming to resemble a long-term campaign of obfuscation and delay. Close inspection of the complaint suggested it would not hold up in court. If the 1980 renewal was invalid, why had Harvey signed it? And if residency at the farm was so important, why hadn't he lived there for the past sixteen years? If joint ownership was critical to the original vision of the farm, how was it that it had first been owned by an individual, Marshall Bloom? And since that individual had given it to the seven members of a trust, why did the opinions of the majority of that trust not outweigh those of a single member?

From the point of view of its planned effectiveness, the complaint looked to the trustees, and some others, simply like a land grab. All other efforts thus far having been unsuccessful, the residents and Harvey had moved ahead to complete what many thought they had been intending all along: to take possession of the farm and at the same time disenfranchise Sam and Janice. To the trustees, this had an added sting: claiming it as their right, Harvey and the MEF wanted the farm for nothing. Thoughts of the self-confident but unaccountable "masked man" described earlier by Peter Natti came readily to mind.

Reactions to the complaint came later, after the document had been read and assimilated, but to keep them in context, it will be best to look at them now. Lazarus reminded readers of the complaint of Harvey's frequent absence during the first years of farm life, and backed up Cathy's view that there had never been a canonical unifying vision guiding the farm. It was not anything to do with organic farming that had brought the original settlers to Montague, he pointed out, but simply a power struggle at the Liberation News Service and the desire to get out of New York. On the issue of absence from the farm among trust members, a matter that would come up again a little later, he joined many in asserting that absences from the farm, as with those of Harvey himself, were common and approved in principle by all involved in farm life.

John, in his response, saw nothing in the current activities at the farm to justify the nonprofit status claimed by MEF, noting that the right to life tenancy for free requested in the complaint certainly sounded like a tangible benefit. Among the several reinterpretations of fact he observed were that by his own admission, Harvey himself had been a prime mover in the 1980 renewal of the trust, and that he was on record as having demonstrated his belief in its validity numerous times. Finally, he noted that it was ironic that Harvey and the MEF saw Janice's use of the garage as illegal, since Harvey himself had lived in it for long periods of time.

Farm family member Chuck Light's lengthy litany of disagreements with the complaint included challenges to the "vision" Harvey and MEF claimed for the farm, to Harvey's vital role there (Chuck noted that certainly this had not been the case during the ten years the farm had been run by Harvey's nemesis, Janice), and to the "pious, self-serving" nature of the complaint's statements—how could Janice have "seized" a building when the community Harvey claimed to represent, at the meetings in 1993 that he cited, had clearly voiced the opinion that she should have it? "Life tenancy!" he ended, evoking its opposite: the endless uncertainty that had plagued most of the farm's inhabitants over the years. You could almost feel his jaw drop.

It was left to the writer in this group, Steve Diamond, to be the most spirited in responding to the complaint. His several pages of comments, addressed to "the honorable presiding judge," and discreetly salted with occasional references to "your honor," "the plaintiff," and "if it please the court" were written in a comic high diction reminiscent of Mark Twain, with touches of the more solemn television attorney Perry Mason, on whose courtroom adventures we had all been raised. As an example of "the chicanery being instigated by Mr. Wasserman and his attorney," Steve pointed out that the nonprofit status so coveted by Harvey and the MEF played no role in the trust as it was written, which for some thirty years had operated instead, for reasons of simple expediency, as a realty trust. As the official administrator of Marshall's estate, Steve continued, he had helped set up the trust based on Marshall's will, explaining authoritatively that "the Realty Trust was itself expressly *not* a nonprofit organization. . . . If it had been part of the will of Marshall Bloom that we form a nonprofit organization, we would have done so as directed by the will." He went on to note that as a voting member of MEF, an organization of his handpicked friends, Harvey was in effect conveying the farm to himself. Steve ascribed that sort of action to Harvey's "mania for controlling the farm" and his decades-long vendetta against Janice and Sam. This "psychological need to control the Farm," Steve said, constituted "a different kind of greed, but just as venal." "In my humble opinion," he concluded, "in many quarters, plaintiffs' activities would be known as 'stealing.'" Apparently no literary buffs themselves, the lawyers for the trustees politely thanked Steve but suggested that the pages remain on file and not be submitted directly to the court.

A Long Month

As January 2001 dawned, then, with a single month to go before the expiration of the trust, several offers for the farm were on the table and numerous discussions about them were being conducted both on and off the record. The trustees awaited official news of the lawsuit initiated by MEF and contemplated the prospect of becoming independent co-owners of the farm. All of these considerations, and a few others, formed the basis for the pattern of overlapping discussions that would occupy them throughout the month.

The trustees' first step following initial news of the complaint was to seek more regular advice from the attorneys they had contacted earlier, going so far as to send a deputation to meet with them in Boston. The initial advice they received was that they offer to sell the farm to those suing them. If this could be accomplished, the attorneys advised, most of the other related issues would become moot. The trustees authorized the attorneys to investigate this route. Their second step, after their visit to Boston and a clearer grasp of the cost of legal representation, was to begin the ongoing task of raising the substantial sums required to afford it.

Next, a week into the month, as this perked, they asked Janice to be clear about whether she still intended to make a firm offer for the farm. She said she did. Lazarus emphasized the need to be explicit and specific. "The time for wishful thinking is over," he wrote. Later in the day, he spoke with her on the phone and was impressed with the plan she outlined. They agreed that she would follow up with a written proposal. In response to Laz's positive report, John asked the lawyers to delay in seeking a settlement with the MEF in order to give the board a chance to consider the plan she was to propose.

The next day, John wrote to Harvey to see whether the two sides could be brought closer together to avoid going to court. Though buffeted by the adverse winds generated by Harvey and the MEF, he was still hopeful that there was room for negotiation. For the remaining weeks of the month, he awaited an answer.

The following day, the trustees turned their attention to their other dissident member, Steve Marsden. Though little heard from, he was respected for his sincerity and compassion. The issues he had raised were relevant and, as the date for the expiration of the trust neared, in need of consideration. Unlike the five-member majority of the board, Marsden, like Harvey, was sympathetic to the current tenants of the farm and felt that they should be allowed to stay. He also believed strongly that no money should be taken for the farm and that it should not be divided, as had been suggested in order to give Janice a place there. Procedurally important in these waning days of the trust, he was convinced that the board, having lived so many years away from the farm, was probably disenfranchised from its role as trustees. The implications of this were that either Harvey was indeed the owner and the others no longer board members, or if he was wrong, that in his view the trust ought to be renewed so that they could again take on their responsibilities.

Most of his concerns could be resolved by formulating a way to express that, as Michael had put forward, care for the farm and its values was not the same as merely living there. A document was drawn up to be signed by all trustees affirming that their mutual absence was an agreed-upon policy. A significant portion of the rest of the month was spent working to convince Steve Marsden that he and they were indeed trustees, and that he should sign this and other measures that would support the trust and avoid the court battle that otherwise loomed.

In view of all this continued ferment, about mid-month Tom Lesser, the local attorney who had always taken an interest in the farm, wrote to the trustees suggesting that the trust be extended into the spring to give the sides a chance to meet and talk directly in the hope of reaching an agreement and avoiding court. The five majority trustees showed interest, though they were quite sure that Harvey would not. It took a two-thirds vote of the seven trustees to substantially change the trust, in this case to extend it. This left the key vote on the matter to Steve Marsden. To that end, another document was drawn up, and persuading Marsden to sign this, too, was added to the trustees' tasks for the month.

At this point, with another prod from Lazarus, Janice presented her written plan. In the kind of homespun language some farm members sometimes used with one another, she asserted that she missed the farm personally and wanted to recapture it for the group. Her hope was that it could be turned into a learning-healing center. She seemed to indicate that she might offer as much as $50,000 per person for the trustees' shares in the farm—far more than the $35,000 figure with which the trustees were then working—and vowed to do whatever was necessary to conclude matters there. She asked for some flexibility with final payments, but did include in her offer taking on what would likely be the ensuing lawsuit from Harvey. Surprisingly, she thought she could work with him and that perhaps together, if they could manage to divest the farm of its current tenants, they might turn it into something suitable to them both. In the inspired hope of adding a bit of humor to the discussion of the farm, and probably of piquing the interest of Steve Diamond, she noted that the complexities of the current situation lent themselves to the development of just the sort of novel he liked to write.

All of this was too much for the action-oriented Lazarus, who, along with John, Michael, and Cathy, had been pushing to conduct the discussion in objective, realistic terms. "Non-specific and downright loony" was the way he described it. In a letter to Steve Diamond, he added "here I refer to her suggestion that Sluggo would agree to evict the current tenants and that the two of them would work together to establish some sort of Arcadian dream!" It did seem a stretch. The upshot was that while the plan in its general form remained on the table and was later modified to be of more use, it was clear that opinion had changed about the wisdom of electing Janice to the board.

This was an interesting moment, revealing some of the intricacies and crosscurrents in the dialogue surrounding the farm. No doubt other factors were at work, but an objective reading of this exchange would suggest that as Janice had grown more comfortable in her conversations with the trustees—old friends, after all—she had let down her guard. By speaking to them in an informal, almost stream-of-consciousness manner, she had revealed the vast differences between her and some members of the board. By now, after a year of serious talks, the five majority board members, all of whom had highly developed abilities and vocations, wanted facts, figures, and an authoritative plan of action. Janice, invoking a more low-key, personal way of relating, cast herself as an heir to the sort of world they had all, in many respects, left behind. As much as the figures she had given or the plan she had suggested, it was probably her manner that convinced members of the board that she wouldn't fit. A few days later, it was clear she would not be elected a trustee. The plan remained on the table, but, as Michael wrote, "What the deal might be is still vague and fluffy."

As a result of the uncertainty of Janice's offer, the lawyers were encouraged to again go back to work speaking with the MEF and its attorney. The farm and the MEF members themselves were soon heard from again as well. In a letter that went out to a large number of the farm's extended family, farm residents restated the beliefs embodied in the complaint, as well as in their ongoing actions: no one should profit from the farm; the trustees do not have a clear claim to ownership; there is hope for mediation; let's look forward to another thirty years of social change. This did have the ring of Harvey to it; apparently, they were learning their lesson well.

Shortly after the arrival of this letter, Steve Diamond wrote in exasperation to his fellow board members about the confused state of current negotiations. He had periodically entered the conversation on behalf of moderation and a peaceful resolution to the farm's problems. His main concern now was to avoid court—with its unpredictable results but quite predictable costs—by way of mediation. His plaintive tone was reminiscent of the police victim Rodney King following the riots we all remembered in Los Angeles in 1991: "Can't we all just get along?" Another recent letter of Steve's had opened "dear friends of the montague conflict association," and went on to recall a relevant truth: "sadly, our history, montague farm itself was born in conflict, and, apparently, we choose to maintain it. . . . it's as if we montagroovians insist on CREATING disorder, disharmony, discordia." Ironically, as he noted, this too echoed a well-known remark from our era, that of Mayor Daley in Chicago in 1968, who famously commented that his police were not at the fractious Democratic Convention that year to contain disorder but to create it. As with other key points in the life of the farm, it was not clear at that moment which side of history we were on.

The current negotiations seemed little different. Of Harvey's role, Steve said, "i think his operation is complete bullshit. . . . the whole thing makes me sick, i must say. . . . i'm so pissed at sluggo, . . . it's like his dream for years has been to be more heroic than sam, something like that, and this is how he has chosen to express it. thus he will be the ultimate hero to this group of youngsters . . . the 'squire' as John used to call him." "Well, this is all a bit surreal," Michael had written to him. "People had said a lot of awful things about Sluggo over the years, but I didn't believe them. Alas." To John, the continuing situation at the farm was "our little Bosnia." Laz wrote, "It's like the Middle East and the farm is Jerusalem. Like it or not the Intifada is on."

Coincidentally, in the outside world—an objective correlative, as students of literature would say—things were turning intense as well. As of January 23, a long, bruising, and to many minds tainted election fight was over and George W. Bush took office as the next president of the United States. This foreboding of things to come did not improve anyone's mood.

As the month moved into its last week, the Lesser plan for extension and mediation was being circulated and voted on. The other plans remained on the table and a few more were added, sometimes in desperation. Michael suggested, for instance, that a number of new people quickly be added to the trust, favorably changing the voting ratio. But Laz immediately noted that most of those he named believed that the farm belonged to the community, and so would not be very supportive of the aims of the trustees. Steve Diamond was briefly thought to be abandoning the group—Sam was his personal attorney and a strong influence—but this turned out to be a false alarm. As late as January 26, John and others were hopeful about extending the trust for the purposes of further mediation. Chuck, noting that the sides were actually fairly close in their terms for settlement, had been corresponding with the MEF about mediation. Through what must have been a very persuasive phone call, Cathy had convinced Steve Marsden to vote for the trust extension. In the interest of promoting peace in the community, the trustees were discussing a lower figure of about $25,000 per person for their shares, to make negotiations easier.

On the 27th, the trustees obtained a copy of the complaint, which they had not yet seen. Its thirty-seven points, reviewed above, removed any doubt about the seriousness of the efforts of Harvey and the MEF. The MEF, for its part, had avoided any substantive discussion with Chuck, further souring the community's hopes for negotiation. By the 28th it was clear to Lazarus that the sides were headed for court. Steve Marsden had returned to his earlier position and, out of what he saw as principle, would not sign the papers resolving the issue of residency at the farm. In light of this, he did not consider himself a trustee, and without his vote the trust could not be extended. Without an extension to discuss it, Tom Lesser had to withdraw his settlement proposal. At some point on the 28th, Susan Mareneck, ever hopeful, forwarded to a large farm list something she thought might make a relevant addition to the discussion. It was the Dalai Lama's "Instructions for life in the new millennium." Instruction number 9 was "Open your arms to change, but don't let go of your values." Number 6 was "Don't let a little dispute injure a great friendship."

On January 31, only a few hours before the expiration of the trust, papers began to be served to the members of its board. They would have twenty days from the last service to reply. "Well, it's happening," wrote John. He asked the five majority members to draft their personal responses to the complaint they had been served and to send off their checks to the attorneys as soon as possible. Laz wrote that he was slightly groggy from the wake he had conducted celebrating the passing of the trust, but noted that he, too, had been served. "What fun," responded John.

9

Annus Luctus (2001)

With the millennial year closed and a new one begun, all took a deep breath and cast a wary eye on the farm's new situation midway through its thirty-third year. The trustees were now co-owners of the farm and no longer bound by the directives of the trust. They were, of course, still morally responsible to the community and the legacy it represented. They were midstream in considering a proposal from Janice and Sam, and they were now headed for court with the new Montague Evergreen Foundation, guardian of the needs of the current farm residents and under the heavy influence of Harvey Wasserman.

The year 2000 had been something of a crash course in postcommunal life. Hopes still remained for the future of the farm, but factions fighting for its control continued to rage and strong opinions remained undampened by the years. New community talents had been applied and undiscovered aspects of personalities and groups revealed.

For the farm community, the year had also constituted an extended lesson in human nature. Bonds that had appeared solid had turned out to be permeable, and principles once unquestioned had seemed suddenly difficult to define or to act upon. Most notably, people had divided themselves into self-selected groups. This was visible, especially in retrospect, in the long-running tug-of-war over the farm, in which, increasingly, the separate parties defined themselves by their strategies: open and straightforward, evasive and devious, clueless, pure.

Surprisingly, much the same seemed to be happening on the national stage as well. As those to the left of the nation's political spectrum absorbed the unwarrentedly partisan presidential loss of Al Gore and the former vice president prepared to reinvent himself as a spokesman for the environment, we noted that, as in our own sphere, the conflict between two avowedly public-spirited members of our generation appeared irreconcilable.

When divested of its at times spurious references to principle, much of the business related to the farm was seen to emanate, similarly, not from the shared experiences much spoken of but from the particular personalities involved. As 2000 had revolved about the machinations of Harvey, 2001 would turn out to be largely about Janice and Sam.

With the change of the board to the status of tenants in common, Janice and Sam had become free to cast themselves more in the role of partners. They remained to some extent outsiders, since their goals were different from those of the former board, but otherwise they were able to use this change to work more closely with the five majority co-owners. There remained also an element of complementarity: The objective of Janice and Sam was, after all, as she had said, to recapture the farm, while the goal of the five co-owners was to divest themselves of it.

In the previous year, Harvey, it appeared, had done everything he could to complicate and delay the decisions that needed to be made about the farm. Sam, in his attempts to slow Harvey and aid Janice, hadn't done much better. Legal tactics had turned out to be Harvey's final line of defense, including the setting up of an entirely separate parallel life for the farm through the new MEF. He had done so much, in fact, that he had pretty much rested his case against the former trustees, having put them in a checked, though not yet checkmated, position. The lawsuit based on the complaint would be the subject of negotiation throughout the year; the current residents were safe until such time as the farm case was decided one way or the other. Farm issues could not be finally concluded until the matters of ownership raised in the complaint were answered, and he had reinforced his bargaining position and made known his bottom-line principles as he saw them, or at least expressed them. Now, with the millennial year passed and a better grasp of the situation and its various players, the co-owners were poised to focus more clearly on the other side of the farm equation.

This first took the form of a revised plan from Janice. In her plans of November and mid-January, she had seemed to be considering offering the trustees as much as $50,000 per person, more than any other bid they were likely to get, and vowed to go to battle to conclude the outstanding legal issues with Harvey. She had asked for flexibility from the trustees—as much as three years or more to pay them for their shares in the farm. Her somewhat scattered, informal letter had closed with the ambiguous admonition "keep breathing, janice." Now, in early February, her approach was a bit more focused. Laz reported from a phone call with her that the per-person figure had become $35,000, with each of the owners getting $5,000 up front. Sam would take over the legal thinking behind their case with the MEF, saving them money on attorney fees. Looked at in a certain light, this was a viable offer. Some of the former trustees, however, saw it as simply a reach for control, and were not pleased at its vague timeline. As one of them remarked anxiously, "I'm afraid that the Sam/Janice proposal looks to me like the moral equivalent of jumping off a cliff."

This offer for the farm was debated over the winter and spring as the group reacted to the lawsuit based on the complaint and discussed appropriate strategies for each. The conversation was conducted both among themselves and with their attorneys, who were preparing a legal response to the complaint for the defendants as a whole, the trustees as well as Janice and Sam. Negotiation and mediation with MEF remained a possibility as well, but with several legal tracks in progress, and the intrusion of delays—the exigencies of personal lives, travel, and other factors—the spring passed slowly. By early July, it seemed no surprise to find negotiations at a standstill, the farm residents uncooperative, and parties on all sides restive.

In late July came another offer from Janice. In March she had retained an attorney of her own in the nearby Amherst area to handle her dealings related to the farm, and now she returned again with another plan. Sensing some of the new owners' concerns about timing and their weariness with the whole farm effort, she moved to a lower figure, but one she could manage sooner, offering them $15,000 per person to be paid

Janice and Sam at the farm reunion discussions, 1993. Photo by Emmanuel Dunand, courtesy FLA.

not in years but relatively soon. This was appealing to the five majority owners, for whom, as the season dragged on, sooner was quickly becoming better. Their animosity toward Harvey, after a year of bruising battle, also led them to feel more comfortable in turning over what would be a five-sevenths share of the farm to the opposing team.

During August this new plan was discussed. Early in the month, John was in touch with Janice to try to push her offer up to $20,000 per person. A week later she replied that she was still consulting with her lawyer about the advisability of her proposal and had been hoping that the owners would be in more of a negotiating mood. The owners had their own thoughts about it: that Janice might have overextended herself and the offer might well be unrealistic.

John was pessimistic and wrote to the attorneys in the third week of August that after months of negotiation and continued uncertainty about the direction of the lawsuit, "the troops are getting a bit restless." He also wrote to Janice, noting that for months things had been moving very slowly at her and Sam's end of negotiations, and not only regarding the finances they were discussing—they had not yet even responded to the complaint, which was holding up work on the lawsuit. He suggested a modified offer of $16,000 per person. In case that didn't come through, he also contacted the attorneys to move forward again on the lawsuit, whether Sam and Janice participated or not.

Janice, who was away, responded the next day, saying that her attorney would speak to theirs about the complaint, and that she would be back in Montague in early September and would be able to do more then. After a few further days of irritation on the part of the owners over this new delay, she replied again. She agreed to the $16,000 figure suggested by John, again with the proviso of some flexibility in the timing of payments. Over the next few days, finances and details were discussed. This seemed to be a deal Janice could live with, and the owners were ready to divest themselves of the farm, even at a reduced price. The mood was hopeful and the attorneys were again asked to put their legal case on hold to provide time for the deal to perk. With the announcement that she again had a new lawyer (the previous one had made a career change and could no longer take the case) and the promise of a contract, if possible, by the end of September, Janice left for Montague, saying that though she would be on the road, she could always be reached through Sam.

Strategies

Why was this significant? Like Harvey, Sam, too, had a strategy. By looking at this period, through the first eight months of 2001, it is clear once again that, as John had earlier set out, the battle for the farm was not about principles and ideals, except in the most abstract way, but about authority, power, and control. Under any of the factions involved—Harvey, Sam, the community, and earlier the trustees—the farm would be likely to remain a countercultural haven of some sort. By bypassing or neglecting any community-based solution, the two individuals involved showed that for each the other remained the true subject of debate.

For Sam, what was beginning to work for him again was the pattern that had served him for years: manipulation behind the scenes. Time was valuable to him, as it was to Harvey, since it allowed for maneuvers and change. (Many in the farm's extended family believed Sam to be behind the long delays following the reunion of 1993.) For this reason he had not been eager to move the lawsuit forward by replying to the complaint and had spoken against the effort to have it decided in a summary judgment as the trustees' attorneys had advised. As the year progressed, what had been presented as the exigencies of deliberation came to look more and more like the now familiar tactics of delay.

Part of the strategic challenge from Sam's point of view was also financial. If for him Janice was the piece in play—no longer a resident and not a trustee, he needed some link to the discussion—any workable game plan had to be within the reach of her resources. Sam could, of course, add to these from his bag of financial tricks, but not without highlighting more of his role than he wished. Some of the moves he and Janice made were thus dictated simply by resource management and were crafted in response to their changing thoughts about it. The figure for the value of shares in the farm went up and down, or the schedule of payments lengthened or shortened, according to their financial thinking at the time or changes that may have recently occurred in their situation or that of the owners.

A related revelation at about this time was that Janice did have resources. As specifics of an agreement were discussed, it came to light that she had a substantial amount of savings, not enough to buy the farm outright but certainly enough for a good start under the right conditions or, as she had called it, a mood of negotiation. This was striking because Janice had always presented herself as something of a victim. Left to run the farm, compelled to take in working, paying residents, forced out of the farm, needing for personal reasons to return to the farm, asking the trustees and then owners for help with this effort—this was the pattern as many of those involved saw it. Under these circumstances, it was strange to find that through all of this, Janice had been accumulating savings—not a bad move, certainly, just somewhat out of character with the rest of her story. It was also believed throughout the farm family that Janice was the co-owner of a piece of land not far from the farm. All of this cast a shadow over her picture of herself as helpless and without adequate resources, and contributed to the question many asked at about this time: Why are we so involved in helping Janice?

The answer was that, intentionally or not, recapturing the farm was—as the trustees had seen from early on—an irrational imperative, a desperate dream shared in different ways by the various groups and individuals involved in its history. Of those engrossed in these dreams, only the community (and earlier the trustees) offered a proposal that might have satisfied—if not perfectly—the competing interests involved, including those of Janice. But the community had no legal standing in the discussion. With this in mind, the strategies of both Harvey and Sam become more apparent. What each was trying to accomplish, it seemed increasingly clear, was in one way or another to secure standing in the legal disposition of the farm. Harvey moved to do this by footing the bill to challenge the ownership of the farm itself and set up its virtual equivalent in the MEF. What Sam now seemed to be doing from the former board side of the fray was simply to buy out the ownership of a large portion of the farm. With this in hand, he would be able to address the challenge brought on by Harvey and the MEF. Because of their sensitive and personal nature, these were strategies that could not be expressed publicly, leading to much of the subterfuge and distraction that characterized the lengthy discussion of the farm.

From their own personal points of view, these strategies made some practical sense, allowing each of them to develop a role in what was to them a very important matter. From a communitarian viewpoint, though, it only underlined the impropriety of their efforts. How could you save a community by ignoring it? What sort of personal drive would excuse overlooking the principles you were committed to defending? Surveying the animosity and the sums of money involved, John wrote despairingly at one point to the other trustees, "This is the price of our youthful dreams."

Would anyone involved in the history of the farm have thought that its situation might ever come to this? Yes. Steve Diamond, for one, had alluded to it when he wrote of the "montague conflict association." Conflict *was* the history of Montague Farm, and attempts to resolve it and to move onto a smoother, more cooperative path generally, in the long run, failed. In theory, of course, it could still be accomplished. Meanwhile, the titans battled on.

Closing the Deal

A week into October, a month after Janice's vow to complete negotiations as soon as possible, a note arrived from Lazarus. *Where's Janice?* it asked in essence; what happened to the deal we were supposed to be working on? He again called attention to the lawsuit and suggested that if Sam and Janice couldn't cooperate, the owners should proceed without them.

As usual, this prodding produced a response. The next day, a new, revised offer arrived from Janice. This time, the up-front money had declined, but the long-term offer had gone substantially up. The latter was to be paid, however, only after the close of the legal battle, possibly years away. Sam was still to oversee the matter in court. This worried Laz: no security was offered for the money due them for parting with their shares, and with differing ideas about the farm, it was not clear whether the owners' interests would be well served by Sam's handling their case. John indicated that he agreed, and that whatever happened with these particular negotiations, the group should again press on with its legal case.

The following day brought a long note from Sam explaining the new strategy that had led to the offer and, at some length, the thinking behind it. This several-page missive, written in Sam's distinctive persuasive style, set out his views on the legal case, the rationale for the recent offer, and, not least, some of the circumstances that had led to its delay. The initial appointment with their new lawyer had taken place in the early morning of September 11, 2001, and run right through the unexpected news of the terrorist attacks in New York. A second meeting a week later had been canceled due to the death of Janice's father. Understandably, he explained, it was not until a third meeting that they had finally been able to develop an acceptable plan.

The impetus for the plan Janice had just introduced, he continued, was to lower risks and to improve the long-term chances of winning a court battle. Sam weighed the various costs and set out his legal reasoning. He contrasted the current proposal to that of seeking a summary judgment, finding their own approach, again, the better of the two. He compared the two cases, that of the owners and that of the MEF, pointing out that though the court costs sounded high, they would be low for the MEF if it won—that is, that the farm could be won in court for far less than it would have cost to buy. Knowing your adversary, in Sam's estimation, was very important. By making it clear that they were taking the long view, he said, their opponents would be warned that they were in for a serious, expensive fight. If we get into this, he concluded, we intend to win.

Interestingly, Sam found the issue of residency—whether or not the trustees had retained their role despite their long absence from the farm—to be the key issue in the case. This indicated that he took the argument of Harvey and the MEF on this point seriously, while among the former trustees it was dismissed as largely spurious.

Reactions to this lengthy disquisition varied. The complexities of the legal reasoning and financial calculations were daunting. The personal and philosophical goals of Sam and Janice were still quite apparent, however, despite the rarefied rhetoric in which they were now expressed. In general, in response, there was a reluctance to rely solely on Sam's analysis, persuasive as it was, or to entirely trust it, since, as John pointed out, both Janice and Sam believed that they had as much right to the farm as did its owners. Unlike Harvey, John noted, they did at least believe that the former trustees owned it, or they wouldn't be bothering to partner in developing a legal case. Cathy, as usual, was on the mark, observing that in Sam's characteristic style his was the only plan worth following. "A crescendo of convincingness and bippety-boppety-boo" was the way she put it.

Lazarus raised another concern. He believed that if the offer was not accepted, the next step for Janice and Sam might be to try to buy one of their shares outright, in order to gain the legal toehold they sought. As the personal attorney of the chronically insolvent Steve Diamond, and a hero of his since the days of the tower, Sam was assumed to have considerable leverage with him. Janice had brought up the subject of Laz's own share with him as well.

This was a prescient observation. A week later, it surfaced that a separate arrangement of some kind between Sam and Steve was being devised. This was, of course, disconcerting, as it would leave a group of only four. While it again confirmed the level of behind-the-scenes machinations that continually revealed itself throughout the course of these lengthy discussions, there was also an upside to this change. Subtracting Steve's share gave Janice and Sam a bit of wiggle room with their figures.

So in mid-October Sam floated a different payment plan. This time there would be much more money up front, freed by the recent deal, but again a lengthy wait for the rest of the new $20,000-per-person figure. Nothing could be done to further this for at least a month, Sam said. Janice was in Korea, visiting her daughter and family. The financial instruments she planned to cash in were in a safe deposit box in Colorado, where she now worked. She would have to stop there on her trip back from East Asia before returning to Montague, when she could again deal directly with the owners. The date for action would be December 7. Probably not coincidentally, this was the birthday of the notoriously superstitious Steve Diamond.

As unlikely as all of this sounded, it turned out to be the basis for a reasonably firm proposal. Over the next few days in mid-October, the owners discussed it, consulted their attorneys, and agreed that it was a fairly sound offer. The principal need, as Laz pointed out, was for a very tight contract ensuring that the owners would be paid under most conceivable circumstances. Of course, as their lead attorney noted, if the case were lost to the MEF, there would be no assets to distribute and no deal to complete. The attorneys felt, though, that the money offered in the proposal was reasonable and enabled their clients to escape the uncertainties of litigation.

Near the end of the third week of October, Sam reassured the group that all was in place, that he expected no further changes, and that the necessary papers would be in the mail to them soon after Janice's return at Thanksgiving. The owners were leaning strongly in the direction of this still-to-be-completed deal. The next day, Janice wrote from Korea to say that she, too, was enthusiastic, and from her perch in the East, sliding back to her earlier and no doubt deeper feelings, compared the fight she foresaw with Harvey to the new and contemporary concern of ridding Afghanistan of the Taliban.

More than six weeks later, and a week after Thanksgiving, the call went out again, this time from Michael. *Where's Janice?* December 7 was approaching, but there was no visible sign of activity. The response from John, still the group's main liaison to their attorneys, was that lawyers on both sides were working out details and were close to finishing the deal.

Two weeks later, John reported that a draft sales agreement had been received by Sam, who was to review it and then forward it to the attorneys for the group. It was Christmas Eve. Prospects for the deal were promising. "Sounds good to me," he wrote, concluding, now perhaps only a little less tongue-in-cheek than earlier, "festively, John."

Three weeks later, halfway into January of the new year, the duly vetted purchase agreement arrived at John's. There were a number of questions on the owners' end, among them issues of potential liability, expenses, and other details related to the court case, as well as special conditions regarding attorney-client privilege. With their lawyers' help they worked through these. As the end of the month approached—marking a year since the expiration of the trust—the group again felt confident that it was on track to conclude its business with the farm, this time through the ministrations of Janice and Sam. Tension seemed to drop, and a sense of impending relief was apparent. Then, a month later, in late February, there was a hint of new developments. In a note to the other majority owners, the full group of five, John wrote: "Word from Sam is that the deal with the Buddhists might well happen."

10

Annus Mirabilis (2002)

The Buddhists? To those not watching the farm situation carefully, this was an unexpected development. Earlier, when Steve Diamond had suggested giving the farm to a group of local Buddhists, the reaction had been surprisingly positive. At the time, almost everyone except those actually living at the farm had considered it a very good idea. As with other good ideas, though—such as the two proposals from the community-based working committee and other calls for sensible solutions to the farm's problems—its proponents had neither acted with sufficient strength nor found a champion able enough to carry it out. It had also been an improbable solution in that the local group probably could not have afforded the necessary renovations, nor was it likely that it would want to involve itself in the complex set of issues that divided the farm family and later sent it to court. Now, however, the idea played itself out in a somewhat different form. The name of the group that many came to hope would save the farm? The Peacemakers. In an interview in 2006, Harvey recounted the story behind this unlikely turn of events:

> As you know, I felt that the nature of the benefit concert from which we took the money to buy the farm mandated that it have a political mission . . . that's one of the reasons I was comfortable turning the farm over to the Zen Peacemakers, which is an international organization focused on promoting peace and social justice.

That was amazing magic; they were a perfect choice. They may have been the *only* choice in the sense that everybody agreed on them. It was incredible. I don't know that there was another group on earth that would have gotten the same reaction. It's as if they were manufactured to take over the farm, and I firmly believed that. Here's how it happened.

Bonnie Raitt's been a friend of mine for a long time. We met in 1978, before MUSE. She is the premiere female rock'n'roll talent of our generation, but she's more than rock'n'roll; she's a magnificent human being.

Bonnie had a husband, named Michael O'Keefe, who achieved immortality by being the son in *The Great Santini*, for which he was nominated for an Academy Award at the age of something like nineteen. He was also the caddy in *Caddyshack*. Hard to top that! Along the way, he became one of the Zen Peacemaker community.

Well, I was agonizing in the middle of hell, you know, that period of what to do about the farm. This is probably in 2001, and—I couldn't make this up—I was at my sister-in-law's house in Columbus. She has two kids, and my kids were there, and we were running around this big family room, and the TV is on, and there's a kids' movie, and I hear this weird noise. It turned out to be a reindeer. There was this crazy kids' drama on the TV, and I look at it, and there is Michael O'Keefe. It was a wacky role. I talked to him about it later. He loved it because he got paid really well. And I said to myself, "Oh, the Peacemakers!" I called him the next day, and I laid out the whole thing, and he said, "They'll never go for it."

So I sent him a copy of Steve Diamond's book *What the Trees Said*, and I said I just knew this was the group. I said, "These are the people, they have got to come to the farm." He said, "No, no, no, they'll never do it." But he sent the book to Bernie [Glassman, founder of the Zen Peacemakers]. Bernie must have read it, and I guess Eve Marko, his wife. They were staying at a gorgeous place in Santa Barbara overlooking the ocean and, you know, why do they need a farm in Massachusetts? —and by the way, they were aware of some of the legal complications.

They were in Santa Barbara at the same time that Steve was

there himself. Maybe he talked to them; I don't know. For the Peace-makers, it was a stretch, but in the end, everybody agreed: it was a miracle, it really was a miracle to find them. We all thought that they were the right group, including the people at the farm. The farmers wound up having their differences with the Peacemakers, but, you know, it was okay, they just wanted to leave finally; they were under such intensive attack, and they wanted to have a place of their own.

The Peacemakers

So as of late February 2002, through the magic of television, or, in farm terms, magic *and* television, the Zen Peacemakers, the eventual buyers of the farm, had appeared on the scene. Besides their right-mindedness they brought to the table a track record of successful projects and, equally important, the fundraising to support them. Even a quick look at the history of the group and its founder confirmed the scope and ambitiousness of their work; through it they had developed a devoted following committed to sustaining their vision. Still, even with the nirvana of a farm successfully transferred to a flourishing Buddhist organization possibly in view, cooperation among the farm family, now in their mid-fifties and midway through the farm's thirty-fourth year, remained difficult to muster. Negotiations continued to sputter and misfire as the rivalry for influence and control moved into a new, more sophisticated phase.

Initially, the Peacemakers' proposal included money for the trustees, as had other offers, and a provision allowing Janice to expand the garage and live in it, as had also been discussed. Further, she was to be allowed access to the conference space they planned to create in the barn, a concept she herself had suggested earlier. The majority group of former trustees also asked that their legal expenses to date be covered. By early March, discussions had evolved to include payments for Janice and Sam. The latter was, perhaps at least symbolically, for his work on the court case, though some sort of payback for earlier legal work for Steve Diamond, or for his long-standing involvement with the farm, were also possible motivators. At this point, the outlay for the Peacemakers to purchase the farm, including all these elements, totaled about

$120,000. The renovations, improvements, and other costs they would certainly encounter would have to come on top of that, raising their total expenses considerably. Still, the purchase figure was only about a third to a half of the farm's market value, so this supportive gesture of the trustees would get them off to a good start.

Over the first two weeks of March, issues surrounding the Peacemakers' proposal were discussed and weighed. What if Bernie Glassman, the Peacemakers' *roshi* and chief dealmaker, were to try to chisel away at the price? (This was one of John's concerns, voiced from his apartment in Greenwich Village.) What if the group later sold the farm and benefited financially from the break in price the owners had given them, and what if those even newer owners were to turn it into condos or a giant yuppie palace? (These were Steve Diamond's perhaps not-so-paranoid fears. He had recently relocated for a brief period to Sedona, Arizona, to do editorial work for a New Age publication.) Had Janice withdrawn the deal they had been working on? (This was one of Laz's concerns. From his home in Florida, he continued to monitor the farm situation. closely. As it turned out, the deal would remain on ice in case negotiations with the Peacemakers should fail.) A general concern was whether Harvey would go along with all this. The conventional wisdom was that having found the Peacemakers himself, and cast himself as an admirer of their work, he would. Steve Marsden? Still somewhat indecipherable, but known to be looking out for the best interests of the farm, as he perceived them. Most felt that the current plan would suit his beliefs.

Other shifting sands included Steve Diamond's frequent changes of mood regarding the proposal, the various players, and the status of Janice in the negotiations. Once Steve's fears had been calmed—most of them could be dealt with by inserting provisions into the deed of sale—he warmed to the idea of the new suitors and began to follow the process more closely. Still, he weighed in with occasional questions and advice as he continued his personal evaluation of the situation. As for Janice, to the surprise of everyone, it was discovered in early March that she had recently purchased a house near Sam in the center of town, some five minutes from the farm. Whether this would have any effect on negotiations was not clear.

Serious Moves

By mid-March there were already clear signs that the Peacemakers were serious. One was that the $120,000 figure floated earlier was becoming increasingly firm. John also reported at this time that Bernie's wife, Eve, also of the Peacemakers, would be flying to Colorado to speak with Janice about the future of the garage. Most promising of all, the Peacemakers confirmed that they would be interested in moving into the farm as soon as mid-June, only three months away. Cheered by their enthusiasm, Steve Diamond suggested an ambitiously early closing date in May. Sam, more cautious, allowed that a July date, Sequoya's birthday, might work. Such proactive measures buoyed hopes all around. There was a new mood of optimism that perhaps after the years of uncertainty, something was actually going to happen with the farm. The peace-oriented Steve Diamond, at times a voluble commentator, earlier in the month had expressed some of this in a long note to Bernie, and to Harvey, that he called "Montague Peace." In its confirmed New Age argot, here in a shortened form, Steve, who generally closed his correspondence "peace to all beings / expect a miracle . . . pass it on . . ." wrote:

> Montague Peace / 3/03/02
>
> I am so thankful that God let me live to see this day: a peace-full future is in the works for Montague Farm.
>
> I have always felt that The Farm, The Land, had a life and a karma all its own separate from the humans and all their *mishegas*— the good, the bad and the ugly. I discovered this early on, that no matter what kind of insanity the free kids might dream up, the land, the "property" (as we white people have come to call it) had its own majesty and magic specific to that place.
>
> I have come to marvel at how God, Spirit, and the Invisible Masters always conspire to "make the right thing happen." Bernie's proposal for Montague Farm, as I understand it from Sam (after he and Bernie met) sounds perfect. It affords a positive result for all parties, even those unborn. The change-over holds the seeds of peace for all humans, and for the "property" itself. (I use quotes here because we all know better.)

Steve Diamond at the farm reunion, 1993. Photo by Emmanuel
Dunand, courtesy FLA.

For over thirty years, the "trustees" did something really amazing—they did nothing.

In the best sense of the word "zen," it seems to me, they allowed
the land, and the people who came to live and learn on it, to run
things themselves!

"Other" trustees might actually have done something, imposed
rules, set regulations, or unleashed their own human Egos on the
Farm. But the Fellowship of Religious Youth's board of seven,
really nine including Sam and Janice, did something remarkable—
they allowed Freedom to rule, for better or for worse, and in this
they performed a noble act. Or should I say a noble non-act?

Moreover, they became trustees at a time when there were no other communes or New Age vibrations for miles around, in a county run by conservative Nixonian Polish American farmers. These "trustees" put their lives on the line in an attempt to create a new way of living. Misguided? Unknown? Different? Risky? Who knew what would come out of it—the magic of our New World Era—but in its unassuming, unheralded way, Montague Farm, and all of us who came of age there, has had its impact.

These trustees then, in 1968, did something that made it possible in 2002 for this property to exist and be available to the Zen Peacemaker Community and its golden work and vision for a peace-full world.

* * *

Montague Farm's elephant in the room has been the war between Harvey on the one side, and Sam and Janice on the other. These three titans have been going at it oh, maybe two decades or so (or perhaps a couple of lifetimes), and it still seems to be bubbling, though we as a tribe don't really talk about it too much. And yet it colors so much—as any kind of war usually does.

In the name of a peace-full future, for the Farm and for the people, it will be wonderful to see them come to the Montague Peace table and sign the accord of 2002.

I know how difficult it is to forgive. But forgive we must. Move on we must.

The future for all of us looks fabulous. Another five hundred years and there will be peace on Earth.

Hey, it's a dirty job, but you gotta start somewhere, someone's gotta do the "heavy lifting." Why not us?

Peace to All Beings, Steve

Such sentiments, verging on the maudlin, could be excused as a natural reaction to the liberating feeling that progress was being made and that lingering issues of our generation were moving toward resolution. Overlooking the statement's self-justification and highly personal views, it did link past realities and future possibilities in a useful way.

There were, however, a number of more difficult, technical matters that required resolution in order to accomplish the dream of peace and an end to the battle of the titans.

Two weeks later, progress was again in the air when Sam produced a draft sales agreement for the Peacemakers group. This, too, had the farm stamp of personal style, but it did outline in fairly clear terms what a final document would need to address, at least from Sam's point of view. Conditions included clearing title to the land (concluding the lawsuit); that the tenants must leave; and that neither the tenants, Harvey nor Steve Marsden would be compensated, as they had all stated was their wish. It established that $20,000 was the necessary payment to each of the majority group of former trustees, plus a total of $5,000 toward their legal fees. Sam and Janice would be paid $10,000, plus another $5,000 for their own legal expenses. In addition, Sam would relinquish his "ownership interest," though it wasn't clear to some that he had one. Janice would receive the rights she wanted to build and live at the farm, though with a new house, it wasn't clear why she would still need them. The rest concerned details of future stewardship and contingencies of ownership (any possible future resale of the farm). The two final conditions were again, as Cathy had once said, "pure Sam": that the signatories "be good people," and that other conditions were to be determined "by mutual agreemint." These overall arrangements were agreed to in mid-April. Soon there was talk of a closing in June.

Before long, momentum began to build. Among the developments: Harvey agreed with the arrangement of proposed payments to the former board, which he had earlier strongly opposed; eventually, in June, he signed his copy of the purchase and sale agreement, an important element necessary to move the entire process forward. Janice, under pressure from her own friends to help clear up old farm business and enjoy her new house, agreed in May to abandon the idea of a toehold at the farm and take a cash buyout instead. Not long thereafter, the ever-doubtful Laz had gained enough confidence in the deal to send in his portion of the sale agreement. This progress was not unaccompanied by further skirmishes, but when the Montague Evergreen Foundation also signed off, along with Harvey, on the first round of their own required papers, John was confident enough to write to the other owners about the state of the deal that "the condition of the patient has improved to guarded from critical."

Staying on Track

There were several sets of papers yet to be signed, however, and further agreements to be reached. By late May, after witnessing further quibbling on the many details in play, Eve Marko wrote to the former trustees that the Peacemakers, dismayed at the high level of discussion and low level of action, were at the point where they needed to know if their offer was going to be accepted, enabling them to buy the farm and meet the most recent proposed closing date of July 1. John reassured her that all was progressing well, and that, as both knew, everyone who would have to sign documents had agreed to do so. Though Laz, understanding the Peacemakers' situation, continued to be concerned, Steve Diamond, ever optimistic and recently returned from a several-week trip to Holland, where he had taken up with a reader of the New Age journal for which he was now working, wrote hopefully to other trustees: "Well, it looks like the party's almost over . . . I'm going to miss all those e-mails . . ." If further conversation was what he wanted, he needn't have worried.

On a Thursday in mid-June, Eve wrote more earnestly. Harvey, Steve Marsden, and the MEF had all long ago verbally agreed to sign the documents necessary to move the sale forward, but none had done so. The Peacemakers in Santa Barbara were now packed and ready to go, with moving trucks scheduled to come in a week and arrival at the farm the week following. They could not move to the farm without a definite promise of ownership—they had made that clear from the beginning. They were not reassured by voices from some in the farm family saying, in the tradition of the farm's "magic," that they should simply make the move and settle the details later. If the promise could not be made, and the necessary signatures be on file by the following Monday, Eve said, they would need to cancel the move and the deal. This would be unfortunate, she added, perhaps as an inducement and an added sign of their commitment, since *roshi* Bernie had recently been successful in raising the substantial funds necessary for the extensive renovations he planned for the farm.

This straightforward approach again provoked a flurry of concerned responses and changes. The day after Eve's letter, the MEF agreed, with various conditions, to sign off on the farm deal. In return for signing away the farm rights many thought they never had, and contrary to their position that no one should benefit from the sale of the farm, they requested a payment of $10,000. Later in the day Steve Marsden and his wife, in their own words and with a somewhat different set of claims—designating the payment as simply a fund enabling them to visit the farm—did the same. Eventually, even the stern-toned Harvey would also accept $10,000, ostensibly for legal work done by his wife, whose services presumably included advising on the plan of delay that had plagued the process for the past two years.

Did this constitute progress? Laz, ever alert, worried that such demands might permanently hobble the deal with the Peacemakers, and suggested it be abandoned in favor of returning attention to the court case with MEF. Eve, however, surprised him by answering, following the critical Monday she had mentioned, that with two of the needed signatures in hand—those of Harvey and the MEF—they would, indeed, go ahead with the move, making a stop in Iowa on their way east for a final, and they assumed successful, negotiation with Steve Marsden and his wife. They expected to be at Montague in late June. Hearing this, Steve Diamond wrote to them confidently, if with perhaps only selective historical memory, that they were "embarked on a beautiful adventure" at the farm.

Soon the process did again appear to be on track. Talk among the owners turned to such more recondite matters as whether their attorney needed to be at the closing; how income gained from the sale of the farm might affect individuals' tax status, how to manage the physical transition at the farm—the changeover of residents, some of whom were not likely to be very cooperative—and the moving target of closing dates and the signatures needed to meet them. While this was a wide variety of circumstances to monitor, most, tempered by the lengthy debate, were now well able to handle such concerns. As the next proposed closing date, July 15, approached battle-weary John advised the owners' attorneys to watch carefully to be sure that all the necessary players would actually be at the closing before arranging to come themselves. "There are some real flakey actors here," he warned. The sale of the farm, an aging commune we hoped was about to see better days, was certainly an unusual event, but, as John said, "although unusual, nothing about this whole affair is usual."

As July 15 passed, the focus for a closing moved to the July 21. While this also failed to occur, it was at least the occasion for some good news—or more accurately, some good, some not. The good news was that the funds for the Peacemakers' purchase of the farm were safely deposited in an escrow account. The lawyer handling the sale, the indefatigable, if at times mercurial, Tom Lesser, advised all concerned that with the funds in hand and the sales contract signed, all the principal pieces for a completed deal were in place. If participants later balked at signing the deeds, the sale could take place in any case, he said, through forced compliance to the sales contract by the court. The other good news from the point of view of many was that the current residents who had constituted the MEF had moved out. The Peacemakers had arrived and it was now time for a changing of the guard. The bad news was that the tenants had not left without a certain amount of friction, bad blood, and, according to some reports, physical damage to the farm. Considering the momentous nature of the situation, though—an entire new era for the farm—most just bit their lips and hoped for the best. From Sedona, the historical-panorama-minded Steve Diamond wrote on July 21, summarizing events in one of his favorite terms, "What a *saga* it's been. . . . Where shall we have the champagne party upon the closing?"

Herding Communards

A week later, there were new developments: In order to meet the deadline for the next proposed closing date, August 15, both Harvey and Steve Marsden would have to sign their deeds, the next step toward completing a deal on the farm without going to court. Both, however, were away on vacation. The nonprofit status of the MEF, it turned out, meant that it could not accept the $10,000 payment it had agreed to with the Peacemakers, so its own new lawyer would have to rewrite that agreement to make the payment directly to its members. The lawyer was also away. The closing date again seemed in question.

The unsigned deeds and further unfinished business raised an alarm bell for Steve Diamond. Was this an indication of further machinations on the part of the dissident owners, Harvey and Steve Marsden, and their friends? Certainly at this point it was not an unreasonable fear. In his mind, even the venerated Peacemakers were not above suspicion. Over the last days of July, Steve Diamond, again exhibiting his penchant for stage managing rather than actually managing, moved closer to the edge of the reservation with a new idea: Why not apply some pressure themselves, as the others had done? From Miami, where he was visiting his parents, he wrote to his fellow owners proposing that they report a bogus offer from an unspecified outside realtor for a much higher figure, thus compelling faster action to complete the deal on the part of the reluctant participants. The ever-attentive Laz calmed him a bit, and the plan, appropriately flamboyant but probably ill-advised, was never launched.

It did, however, play into the general tensions mounting. Steve, as he wrote to the others, had developed enough confidence in a coming deal that he was beginning to plan the next phase of his life (presumably including more trips to Amsterdam) on the basis of his share of the harvest from the sale of the farm. The closer it got, the more tantalizing it became. When obstacles arose, he increasingly took umbrage at those involved. For Laz, it was another wake-up call to keep things on track. Long disabused of any romance of the farm, he, like the other majority owners, simply wanted to be out from under its demands and potential liabilities, and, of course, with some reason, had no objection to any financial benefit that might result. Increasingly, he took a hard line in order to finally wrap up all business concerning the farm.

The tension remained in the air when the next round of contingencies arose. It became clear that Harvey and his allies, before they would sign any further documents, wanted written guarantees for matters that had not yet been committed to paper. These included a provision in the contract ruling out subdivision and sale by the Peacemakers, and a written statement of Janice's buyout agreement giving up any property rights at the farm. From the viewpoint of Harvey and his team, these were long-standing conditions. They seemed to constitute a reasonable request. Somehow, perhaps through miscommunication, they had not been completed earlier. Again, Laz looked into this and wrote a memo to the other owners explaining what needed to be done, noting that the closing date was once again likely to be delayed.

While this seemed a helpful clarification, Laz viewed it differently. As lawyers changed, vacations wreaked havoc on any potential progress, new demands developed, the closing was moved back, and communication continued to prove difficult, Laz concluded, as had Steve Diamond, that Harvey and his group were reveling in the confusion and had no intention of completing the deal. Meanwhile, he noted, the Peacemakers had been at work at the farm and, as he reported, had "irrevocably altered the property, pulling down parts of and seriously remodeling the barn." They also "do not seem inclined to attempt to enforce the Purchase Agreement," that is, to take the route through court if crucial signatures and approval were missing.

By early August, despite the progress that had been made, Lazarus was clearly frustrated and without any new tools to apply to the situation. Writing to Tom Lesser, he set out the current need, insisted on by Harvey, to rewrite certain provisions of the purchase agreement, implying his own impatience with the entire process. Lesser replied that he was on a much-needed summer vacation but that, as he had earlier assured them, all was in place for a closing when he returned. The main issue now holding things up, he wrote, was resolution of the lawsuit brought by the MEF challenging ownership of the farm, since its title had to be cleared for it to be sold. The same day, John, returning from a vacation of his own in the Catskills, concurred that despite occasional setbacks, things at this point seemed to be "going as well as can be expected."

Ten days later, at midmonth, the pressure had built even more. Citing the next proposed date for closing, August 26, Laz worried that it, too, might pass unheeded. The contract still hadn't been rewritten, he pointed out, and Harvey continued to add a note of uncertainty by questioning its legitimacy. In addition, Bernie Glassman and Eve Marko would be traveling and away from the farm until nearly that date, making any further negotiations or clarifications more difficult. "For myself," he wrote in warning to the other owners, "I am quickly losing patience. . . . Unless things do change, and very, very soon, you all should know that I am prepared to depart . . . and pursue several legal fronts of my own." He would, of course, he added, since his mission was to inform and not to threaten, consult them first.

The following day, Steve Diamond wrote to Harvey asking directly if he intended to follow through to complete the deal with the Peacemakers. "ABSOLUTELY POSITIVELY," Harvey wrote back, abandoning his lower-case style for good measure. As he had at other points, he blamed the configuration of the original trust for most of the problems they were experiencing, and asked again for written confirmation that his conditions had been met. Echoing Steve's closing, "Peace Day January 1 Every Year / expect a miracle . . . pass it on," he signed off, as always, "No Nukes, Sluggo."

Later in the day, Laz wrote to the other owners, summarizing the situation. He seemed to feel a bit better about it, but warned that they still had some key issues to address and should remain engaged in the process in order to meet the upcoming deadline for a closing. Harvey's legal team, he reported, was back in place and was working with him to amend the final contract. Janice's buyout papers were being faxed to him as proof of that transaction. Most intriguing to some was a new covenant to be written into the deed. This was, Laz said, a buyout option for the working committee. To protect the larger community's interest in the farm, they were to be given first refusal in the event that the Peacemakers either failed or chose to sell the farm. Also crucial now was the special agreement that had been reached with Steve Marsden in Iowa in June. It was discovered that the Peacemakers had never written it up, and without this document in hand Marsden would not sign the final papers. A few further details were dealt with in this letter, all pointing to a closing in late August, now only some ten days away.

In answering Laz's letter, Steve Diamond called the circumstances surrounding the current situation of Steve Marsden "a strange curve ball from left field," but this was not really the case. From the beginning of the long discussion on the farm, Steve Marsden had made it clear that he would follow his own principles and both the letter and the spirit of the farm as best he understood them. He had gone to considerable trouble to try to understand the trust document and to envision projecting its original purposes into the much later present, and he had often asked for clarification on various points. He was at a disadvantage for living

Steve Marsden at the side door of the barn, 1969. Photo by Peter Simon, courtesy Beech River Books.

far from any of the group of owners and being more detached from them
than even Laz, who, once found, had immediately begun to engage the
key issues and personalities in play. He was also at a handicap in that his
literalism and disinterested idealism could not really compete with the
highly interested, more creative practical approaches taken by the principals on the major sides of the farm debate. The truth was that he had
set out the conditions on which he would agree to the sale of the farm in
a document he had submitted months earlier. Because of the peripheral
status others had assigned him in the deliberations, however, his views
were never completely addressed—though John, Michael, and Cathy had
all valiantly tried—and the document he had produced was never signed.
In a sense, this was another reflection on farm life, in which, historically,
the most tenacious always seemed to survive, while the reasonable, cau-
tious, considerate, or thoughtful more often did not.

It was also relevant that both Steve Marsden and his wife were working during this period, and found little time or support for their part
in the arduous battle for the farm. They used a public fax machine and
borrowed time at their workplaces to communicate. Their life posed a
great contrast to those of Sam and Harvey, both full-time communicators with networks and infrastructure to rely on, and also to those of the
other owners who were by and large well traveled, more worldly, and
relatively secure. In a curious way apparently unappreciated or perhaps
strategically ignored by the others, Marsden and his wife were probably
the strongest link in the discussion to the farm's actual past as we had
known it.

Off The Rails, Then Back On

A week later, with only four days to go until the proposed closing, Laz
wrote in suppressed agitation to Bernie and Eve of the Peacemakers,
then in Hawaii for at least another week. Had they settled with Steve
Marsden? Would there be a closing, as scheduled? What other problems
remained to be addressed? The answer from Eve, if not what he wanted,
was probably what he expected. It was headed "Delays." The attorneys
were still talking, and two important papers, the deeds from Steve Marsden and the MEF, were not yet in. The Peacemakers had done all they

could, she wrote. In each case, the document had been promised weeks before but not yet submitted. She wasn't sure where to turn to resolve this. Tom Lesser had felt that a closing at the end of the month, a few days after the 26th, might be possible, she said, but first the two signed deeds would have to be in hand.

"Time is up," Laz wrote abruptly, in response, to the four other majority owners, "I'm off the reservation." Turning to hardball tactics himself, he was going to reclaim his deed, resign from their joint legal representation, and move to evict the Peacemakers. He would then have a court-appointed master oversee the property, and pursue the legal case in court.

Once again, a great scurrying and commotion was heard. Twenty-four hours later, Laz again wrote to the four other owners, this time in a more settled mood. Firmly convinced that all was in place for a closing on Friday, August 30, Lesser had asked him to put off for a week his doomsday scenario, which would undo all their efforts over the course of the year. Having spoken to the Peacemakers and become convinced that they were doing all they could, and with no one wanting to return to battle with Harvey and his forces, Laz had complied. Again, the end seemed close. This time, if they did not succeed, the only remaining prospect was, in one form or another, the courts.

In the meantime, Eve revealed a surprising new development. For unknown reasons, Tim and Lise, stalwart believers that no one should profit from the farm, had decided they wanted a larger slice of the spoils from the Peacemakers sale. No figure was named, but a meeting had been arranged, and the following Wednesday, two days before the closing, they were to get together with Bernie and Eve on their return from Hawaii to work out a new and larger payment in return for their willingly having left the farm. That was five days away; all hoped it would end in a positive resolution.

With everything in suspension, and the champagne Steve had facetiously ordered on hold, history stepped in, as it had so many times with this group. Word had gotten out of the Peacemakers deal; an article appeared in the local paper chronicling the history of the farm and noting the continuity represented by its potential new owners. Comparing the farm's scrappy past with its upbeat, savvy future, the reporter contrasted the pile of discarded metal and old appliances lying outside at the farm, symbolizing its former life, with the half-dozen shiny new Macintosh-equipped workstations that had been installed by the Peace-makers, "a global, multi-faith activist network," in the office section of the newly converted barn. The new owners, it said, had an agreement with the farm's trustees to close on the sale by September. Steve Diamond, identified as one the farm's trustees, told the reporter "I see it as fortuitous." Publicly, the die had been cast.

Indeed, a day later Steve himself reported in from Montague. "I'm here," he wrote; "I believe the closing will be this week." If there were ever a sign that the farm business was going to be completed, this was it. The lure of the honey pot was too strong, and Steve was on the scene to make sure it appeared. He used all his effort as on-the-ground representative of the former trustees to help conjure it up. Working to mediate and enable, he actively prayed for a positive outcome and started signing his e-mails "Gandalf."

But it was not yet the end. The following six days would include a rare letter directly from Bernie asking Harvey and his team to live up to their earlier agreements and sign whatever papers were necessary to complete the deal, and a lengthy response from Harvey to Steve Diamond bemoaning the time, effort, and money expended on the farm effort and placing all delay over these months squarely on Steve's own shoulders. The case he made revolved around misplaced communications of various kinds and Steve's earlier insistence on giving Janice a permanent place at the farm, a matter that had been resolved months before. Reading this note, one would have thought Harvey the victim of this protracted process, not one of its principal instigators. This period extended right up until the closing. Pertinent personal information from all involved, which had somehow never been assembled over a half year of serious negotiations, had to be quickly gathered and faxed, and on the day of the closing itself, there was a tense wait for the arrival of the final papers from Steve Marsden, in Iowa, said to have been sent by express mail but not arriving until minutes before the meeting itself—the last piece of the puzzle.

Finally, on August 30, came word from Steve Diamond:

yes, darlings, the checks are in the mail, going out today. closing happened at high noon, uneventful, nice. bernie and eve and the peacemakers would have been hand picked by marshall, i tell you, it's absolutely uncanny. they are good people and their work is righteous. so all in all, it's fucking remarkable.

congratulations, james, your readiness to end the charade made it come to a happy conclusion. i also waved gandalf's wand, and altogether, a successful close.

now, about that champagne. . . . peace to all beings, stevie

11

The Farm and Its Legacy (2002–2006)

On a recent visit to the farm, I considered the changes that had come to it and reflected on the path both the farm and its inhabitants had traveled. As the new Peacemaker Circle International, the farm that had reluctantly accepted electricity, plumbing, and a telephone now had a website of its own. The summer kitchen of which I had once been so proud was gone; the cabin I had built was in ruins. But the barn where we had milked cows and created simple furniture from reclaimed boards was now a state-of-the-art meditation and conference center called the House of One People. Local conjecture suggested that nearly a million dollars had gone into its renovation and the reconfiguring of the surrounding land.

Looking at the farm in view of its changes and history, it seemed to me that its true legacy was as an embodiment of ideals, of reaching some tangible level of success in leading a life of independence from expectations and routine, and as a bellwether for political, cultural, and social change. Certainly it had had a number of successes—the activism, environmentalism, and role as an agent of social change for which it was known. But, looked at in another light, it had clearly failed in several of the highest goals it was thought to represent. It had failed to support some of its neediest individuals; it had failed to create a sustainable community; and looking at the world in recent years, it seemed to me that it had failed to engage the nation it had sought to sway, in an influential way, in some of its core beliefs. Some of the progressive agenda of our era had of course prevailed and even been assimilated into American and international life—especially in matters of entertainment, dress, and style of life—but in a world still in thrall to class, war, race, consumerism, and many of the other causes we had taken on, the best that could be said, perhaps, is that we had won some battles, but certainly not the war.

Really, I concluded, the farm was a naive organization, one that did not strive to evaluate or promote its own success in any calculated way. That was as it was intended to be. We were never a doctrinaire group with a list of tasks posted on the fridge or a long-range agenda. If the farm was a victim, I felt, it was, like other experiments of its time, the victim of its own unfettered style and unfocused beliefs. As with most such organizations, its wounds were often self-inflicted. It was also a casualty of other, largely unavoidable factors: the youthfulness of its original members, its philosophical resistance to mustering its resources, and the complex times through which it had endured.

Individuals who left the farm had often continued in the succeeding years to follow their beliefs and, despite the usual obstacles, generally found their own way. But for those who remained, being bound to the farm or its sister organizations posed difficult questions. What was the purpose of the farm? To whom did it belong? Who should pay its bills, or benefit when they were paid? Who had rights and authority there, and who did not? The free-form, idealistic outlook of the farm offered no structure to deal with such issues, no method to turn belief into practicable reality.

Times have changed, though, and some of the ideals of our era have indeed been incorporated into American culture, and often beyond. Did the farm and its family play a role? I think so. When larger themes are considered—romanticism, activism, social issues (love, money, leadership, property, work), and others—I think it will be seen that the farms in their influential years were an island of sanity of a certain sort, though to many they did not appear so at the time. Their legacy is the important American one of the value of contrarianism and independence, a stance that is all the more important the harder it becomes to sustain. There is, however, another side to this ideal. As I point out to literate friends who ask why I left a place considered an Eden some forty years ago: We all like to glean important cultural lessons from Thoreau, but Thoreau chose to live by himself at Walden, not with his friends at Brook Farm.

Over the next few years, some wounds healed and the Peacemakers made themselves at home. Only a year after the long-delayed closing, the House of One People (HOOP) opened for use. Early members of the farm were invited; the Peacemaker community honored them as "elders." Soon after that, the Peacemakers were offering a full slate of programs and had developed a distinct local identity of their own. Clearly, a new era had begun.

In February 2006, four years after their first appearance, the Peacemakers held a community service in the large public HOOP space. The mission was to introduce the public and the extended farm-Peacemaker family to the organization's newly completed home and renewed institutional life. Both Harvey and Sam were publicly thanked for their roles— Harvey for alerting the Peacemakers to the possibility of the farm, Sam for helping smooth their way once they arrived. Some of the best known of the Peacemaker community from around the country were there; the mood was upbeat and positive. The news making its way around the room that day, however, as the crowd assembled, was of someone who was not there. In hushed tones, members of the farm's extended family were noting the passing of Steve Diamond, who had died of heart failure earlier that morning.

This confluence would certainly have pleased Steve, who had written of how glad he was to live to see the future of the farm put into responsible hands, and whose belief in the significance of synchronicity was never-failing. As the final ceremonial strand to tie together his life, dying at the moment of the renewal of the farm he had helped found, and then to bring to public attention through his book *What the Trees Said*, would have seemed entirely logical and heaven-sent. This did not go unnoticed by the farm family in attendance. In May, a service for Steve was held in the HOOP space, its first use by the "elders" who had tamed it in their youthful days, but now inhabited it only as aging visitors. This, too, brought to mind thoughts about the farm and its fate.

If the farm Steve had helped to envision had indeed been a victim of its own style and beliefs, how had this been allowed to happen? Wasn't

Steve Diamond in the upper field at the farm, 1970. Photo by Peter Simon, courtesy Beech River Books.

there something of a more instructive nature to be said about this? And how could the unbridled idealism and enthusiasm of the farm's early days in the 1960s have altered course so conclusively as to lead to its dissolution? The farm seemed to be in good hands, but why was it no longer in ours? It was to address such questions that I had set out to complete the story begun some thirty-five years before.

Points of Reference

As with any number of other issues we had encountered, the answer to this was complex and not always easy to discern. Certainly the farm had been born in idealism. The moment Steve had described so well in his book, in which Marshall had suggested moving the Liberation News Service to a farm in the country, replacing the frayed ties of intense movement conflict with the soothing familial balm surrounding Kurt Vonnegut's concept of the karass, had exemplified an important transition among youth from protest to demonstration, from negative objection to positive, prefigurative action. It's hard to imagine, especially at that time of ongoing social and political conflict, anything more hopeful. But from that point on, the farm had evolved largely on its own through a series of stages that had lasted nearly thirty-five years—far more than any of its twenty- to twenty-five-year-old inhabitants could possibly have imagined. From an urban political organization, it had briefly become a rural one. It had then evolved into a back-to-the-land commune and organic farm and then an active center for the antinuclear movement, before devolving again into its earlier rugged struggle for survival. After the mid-1980s, and certainly again by the mid-1990s, one could fairly have asked, as the cartoonist Robert Crumb had asked of the older generation before us ("*This* is a system?"): What had become of the magic of the farm and its family?

This was the vulnerable state of the farm as Harvey and Sam began to focus on it more intently in the waning days of the trust. Whatever the source of their conflict, both personal and philosophical, it, too, had had time over these years to develop and change. In the beginning, these two people, so similar in their goals and relative levels of energy to pursue them, had worked together in a mood of mutual respect. It wasn't long, though, before cracks in this potentially ideal partnership had begun to appear, eventually leading to their differences over the MUSE organization and then over the future of the farm. In the early days, Sam had already begun to see Harvey as the "squire" of our small estate—as Steve Diamond had humorously styled him in *What the Trees Said*—spending excessive amounts of time walking the property lines of the demesne and living far too much, in Sam's opinion, by his own lights. Harvey, for his part, had taken a dim view of Sam's self-guided efforts to influence the community along lines of his own. On one day in the farm's early history Sam and others reported to those at dinner on the considerable energy they had spent fencing the farm pasture, in order to raise beef for the table. Harvey, intent on converting the other farmers to his recently acquired vegetarianism, announced that he had torn it down.

In other circumstances, such confrontations might have been subsumed into the daily life of the institution they both loved. But the farm as it developed was instead an ideal seedbed for the propagation of such differences. Over a series of conversations, I investigated these ideas with Susan, who, of course, knew all the players and had a good grasp of the long history of the farm. She pointed out that in the borderless, ill-defined life of the farm, issues could continue unresolved for years. As people came and went and philosophies evolved, as individuals found their own way, often irrespective of the trajectory of others, pressure surrounding unresolved issues could build until they either exploded or were simply submerged. The result would be minor reorganization and resumption of the life that had gone on before. It wasn't until the looming deadline of the expiration of the trust, she suggested, that some of the long-simmering matters surrounding the farm had had to be confronted, leading to the fireworks that followed.

She noted, as well, something I had seen in passing but had not been able to formulate adequately. Despite the congruence of many of their political views, Harvey and Sam had differing philosophies of how to enact them. Harvey, she pointed out, leaned toward larger organizations and national- and international-scale approaches to the political and social problems he pursued. Sam, in contrast, believed in employing a grass-roots local- and community-level route to reform. This difference certainly rang true to me. Harvey, though he had lived at the farm, had

eventually returned to his midwestern city, found a home at the nationally and internationally active Greenpeace, and continued to publish and
speak to the extensive audience he had developed. Sam, though he had
run large organizations, crisscrossed the country in the service of nuclear
power, and lived in the city, had eventually returned to Montague, first
to the farm and then the small town nearby. His actions, for the most
part pointedly not public, tended to be of a one-on-one nature. Because of
the malleability of the farm environment, these two outlooks had continued simultaneously, uninterrupted by each other, for years.

As I mulled over these insights, I came to see another. Harvey and Sam
were often described in terms of their evident egos. That much was obvious, despite their avowed preference for a leaderless community. But they
were really more than mere egotists. Presenting themselves as important
proponents of community, equality, family, environment, health, clean
politics, and other indisputable goals, they accrued to themselves trappings of authority and power that went beyond the personal. This was
beginning to sound familiar. What was it that it reminded me of?

As the *Iliad*, the classic text of Western conflict, opens, it is the wrath
of Achilles and his quarrel with Agamemnon that occupy center stage.
But the background, the critical area of motives and movers, is occupied,
significantly, by the gods. In today's terms, the role of the gods might
well be equated with that of psychology. How does anger come about?
How do we understand others' reaction to it? How do we explain its
unpredictable results? These are questions that have fascinated mankind
for centuries. Our answers today may differ from those of earlier times
in their personnel, but not in their content.

In looking back over the puzzle of Harvey and Sam and the farm, it
seemed to me that perhaps this was the missing piece. Though probably
neither of these two figures would care to admit it, the farm situation, I
thought, had moved them into territory in which, as with the legendary
heroes Achilles and Agamemnon, their anger had put them beyond the
reach of objectivity or sensible thought, and thus out of their own control.
(This is something the trustees realized early on but with the battle
already raging could do little to defuse.) Thus, the farm situation swept
on, continuously growing in intensity, but with nothing short of the
death or complete surrender of one of the parties to stop it.

From this, a crucial element in the battle between Harvey and Sam comes into focus. They had both overstepped the bounds of reason but would not—probably *could* not—retreat. This helps explain one of the central conclusions I reluctantly drew concerning this protracted affair—that the two people most invested in keeping the farm intact, and who had most expressly tied themselves to its history, values, and potential future, were actually the principal cause of its eventual loss. Certainly, in any rational frame of mind, this was not something either of them would have contemplated, leading to the unavoidable conclusion that their actions were, frankly, irrational. (John Wilton had harped on this in his messages numerous times.) The conclusion to the long farm battle confirms this. Each of these figures was so intent on the other not winning the valued prize that they both ended up cooperating to turn it over to a third party.

Furthermore, looking at the fine print of the deal through which this was accomplished, I realized something else. Would we expect participants in a thirty-year-long battle that neither had won to simply fold their tents and go home? Probably not. By allowing the inclusion of a first-refusal buyout option in the sales contract for a community-based group such as the one led by Susan, all involved in the sale of the farm acknowledged that, as solid as the Peacemakers looked, this might not be the last chapter of the conflict. Should the Peacemakers choose to move on, as they had from Santa Barbara, or fail, as numerous such groups had, or fall victim to the sort of infighting that had always plagued idealistic residents of the farm, the entire issue might arise again. In the back of my mind, I reserved a small spot to remember that should this occur, the sides clearly remained ready to return to battle, and that somewhere in their own minds, Harvey and Sam were each probably sifting names for a new board to oversee the farm, should it be needed.

It's not hard to translate the elements of classic wrath to the story we've just seen. Yet while in our telling the death and celebration of Steve Diamond provide closure to the story, the battle of the titans has no such poetic justice or ceremonial aspect to bring it to an end. And so, as with much of life, the actual story as it was enacted is far messier than the one told here through art.

But the lesson from this period perhaps most pertinent to the larger

Turtle Island Design
Architectural Solutions with the Environment in Mind

The new House of One People in the farm's converted barn, 2002. Jeremy Toal,
Turtle Island Design.

farm family is not mentioned in the *Iliad* at all. For Odysseus, the multi-
talented Greek hero who has remained over the years such an important
model for the value of the individual, the ten years following the long
siege of Troy were spent in something of a daze wandering back toward
his island kingdom, wife, and son. This was the experience of many in
the farm family, left to wonder what those years were all about and, in
some existential way, working to find their way home.

Transcendent Anonymity

In the course of trying to better understand the characters of Harvey, and, especially, Sam, I also turned to the work of Joseph Campbell,
whose *Hero with a Thousand Faces* includes many references to the trickster. The trickster of anthropology and myth is a fascinating figure, usually human, but with mystical tendencies. The trickster has what Campbell calls "a transcendent anonymity," a view of himself as inhabiting a

lofty place beyond "self-centered, battling egos" mired in mere time and humdrum human affairs. Donning a costume or a mask, he goes where others cannot, indulges in arcane adventures, and employs cleverness to pursue great tasks for his culture, acts that help or guide those around him. Unfortunately for these others, he often shows them little respect, since his strategies and actions are far above anything they themselves can perform. As Campbell comments, this hero is preoccupied with his mission. If those in the world want him, they must seek him out: "Society," he says, "will come knocking at the door." From my experience, this struck me as a good description of Sam.

The feats that can deliver high-stakes benefits to the community require extraordinary capacity, self-confidence, and often cunning. In the story of the Yoruba trickster figure Edshu, as Campbell recounts it, observing two farmers in adjoining fields, the trickster walks between them with a hat painted in two colors, one on each side. The resulting conflict of perception—each of the two legitimately seeing a different color—sows immediate discord. Indeed, says Campbell, for the trickster, life is "a vast, horrendous Divine Comedy," and his laugh is one "with the hardness of life itself." A corresponding, balancing assurance, however, supported by the presence of larger, guiding forces, lifts the overall outlook of the trickster to the transcendent anonymity Campbell had noted: someone controlling perception but safely disguised from being revealed in that role. Again, for me, Harvey and Sam came to mind.

Such figures of transcendent anonymity include sages and wandering mendicants, the princely beggar, the bard, or the masquerading god. This unknown knower's role provides a satisfying position, but it's not easily compatible, I thought, with the normal lives of other people.

Reviewing this literature opened an important perspective on some of the characters here. Echoes of godlike behavior certainly helped explain the larger-than-life quality they exhibited. The quasi-religious, moral forces invoked provided another helpful clue. Such figures often present themselves, as did these, as agents for matters of overwhelming importance. Fire. Water. Life. Safety. Happiness. Health. Community. With ideals like these, it's difficult to deny the ministrations of those who present themselves as their champion and intermediary.

In viewing the trickster, a character type began to emerge: a powerful personality with a manic energy directed at some specific target or cause. The seriousness of the mission puts him (or her, because this is not a gender-specific profile), in his mind, above other people, even if he is unwilling to acknowledge it. The importance of the cause defended or pursued offers the cloak of great assurance Campbell describes; as we say today, it's the right thing to do. This is someone willing to take on great tasks and to guide others. Because he acts in their name, he sees himself as selfless. If ego is a danger, it is a disease that, in his own view, he has been miraculously or by moral association, inoculated against.

Yet—how to lead and not lead? Here is where all the odd qualities arise that make such people so difficult to understand in the context of daily life. In their own eyes, they resemble the Eskimos' Raven, the unassuming rural community member willing to don the appropriate guises to—in our world, let's say—jive in Los Angeles with the rock stars on one day, meet in New York with the attorneys on another, and on yet another shut himself in his office in old sweats to mull over strategies and goals. And, perhaps more challenging, to later remove those guises and attempt to live the life considered normal by friends and peers.

Given the stress and demands of such a life, it's not surprising that some of its structure might bend, that it might even be useful for it to be flexible to accommodate the contradictions built into it. God or man? Leader or equal? Work or play? Rewarding or just satisfying? These are questions few can answer—perhaps in conventional terms, they are not answerable at all. Recall Edshu: obfuscation, chaos, laughter—useful tools of the disingenuous. These are ways of managing others while protecting oneself—to lure them off base in order to maintain a quasi-regal control over one's missions of great importance.

Looked at in this way, some of the attitudes Sam and Harvey brought to the farm battle become apparent. They were above it, and thus less accountable. Their views were based on lofty aims, and so in each case inalterable. (Factions tend to differ on the *facts*, as they see them, and thus often prove irreconcilable.) Their penchant for manipulation, obscured in various ways, created a minefield difficult for others to navigate. Their refusal to deal squarely with each other (angry, battling gods) led to labyrinthine ploys and negotiations that worked directly against the community they were, each in his own way, and by his own account, trying to save.

A Contemporary View

Of course, there is no need to go as far afield as ancient epic and anthropology for sources to inform the farm story. In her 1991 book *Political Protest and Cultural Revolution*, a study of nonviolent direct action in the 1970s and 1980s, the historian and theorist of social change Barbara Epstein devotes an entire chapter to the farm-related Clamshell Alliance. Her perceptive analysis, focusing on issues surrounding governance and authority in a democratic organization, shows that the difficulties faced by the Clamshell Alliance strongly foreshadowed the later ones at the farm—a situation not only parallel in content but actually created by the same people.

In analyzing the problems that developed in the Clamshell Alliance, Epstein notes a range of issues very similar to those later faced at the farm: an organization founded in idealism and operating on the model of a leaderless democracy falters under the influence of entitled leaders challenged by a group of activist insurgents. In the case of Clamshell, organization founders and stalwarts held undeclared reins of power that were later challenged by a set of new recruits intent on more overtly radical action. In an important misstep—the matter of the Rath proposal offered by the state of New Hampshire—the self-enabled leaders transgress the philosophy of the organization, jeopardizing its future. Epstein makes several points about these circumstances:

The importance of community: Democracy was at the center of the Clamshell Alliance's appeal. As Epstein notes, people joined the organization to be part of a "community of resistance," to unite with others to make their views be heard, to work together to make a difference. When community failed, so did the organization.

Problems of governance and organization: There were limits to the consensus process of decision-making. When problems emerged, the organization was too cumbersome to respond. Conflicts were allowed to simmer: "In an organization which officially had no leadership" Epstein writes, "no one had the authority to intervene."

The aging of institutions: Such problems mattered less when the organ-

Tony Mathews (*center*) and others, Packer Corners Farm, May Day, 2008. Photo by Jennifer Ann Fels.

ization was young. While enthusiasm was high, anything seemed possible and compromise was relatively easy. (In an inspired example, Epstein describes early Clams solving one of their logistical problems very simply with some cardboard boxes.) As the life of the organization became more complex, simple spontaneity and loose organization no longer served.

Dealing with change: The new hardliners who moved into the Clamshell Alliance had no stake in arriving at consensus. They saw their differences as being based on principles, and principles were, on both sides, nonnegotiable. Direct action had worked for Sam, the "tower-toppler," but the same kind of action now advocated by others did not fit the long-range strategy he had later helped to develop for the group.

Outright clashes: Epstein believes that in the case of the Clamshell Alliance, it was irresponsible for the leadership to step in with its own ideas.

When the principles of an organization are violated, she suggests, the organization is likely to suffer. In the case of the Rath proposal, agreed-upon procedure was, she says, violated "in both form and spirit" in only "an arm-twisting type of consensus." The resulting decision "effectively destroyed the Clamshell."

Why would these matters come up? As Epstein points out, young organizations are rightly fueled by optimism and ideals—the "magic" endorsed by both the farmers and the Clams. But for the farm-based leaders of the Clam, this early spirit came back to haunt them. The early days of the Clam were, indeed, magic, as Harvey has related and Epstein concurs. But, she adds: "Magic doesn't last." Pointing to the addictive, intoxicating nature of civil disobedience, she notes the difference between moral witness and political efficacy. Quoting longtime pacifist Marty Jezer, ironically a farm-family member, she makes the point that moral witness and civil disobedience as a tactic do not translate easily into a lifestyle or the model for an organization.

To some extent all of this was true for the farm as well, though the events were spread out over many years in a more complex way. Certainly, as I view it, just as with Clamshell, self-declared leaders of the farm—Harvey and Sam—impeded the will of a larger community, eventually leading to the loss of their idealistic joint endeavor. As Epstein puts it, when the philosophy of a community is transgressed—in this case, allowing community values to be overshadowed by ones largely personal—its existence necessarily comes into question.

And similar to the case of Clamshell, when problems did appear, they were allowed to fester. As an organization, the extended family of the farm was too cumbersome to respond. Its years of spontaneity were behind it, and no new entity or agreed-upon leader had emerged to move it forward. Indeed, of those who took on the role of leaders some of the key players had, as Epstein recounts of the Clamshell Alliance, little motivation to agree at all, being focused instead on winning their own battle of purported principle.

Of course, others were at fault as well. The community was unable to rally, largely because much of it had moved on and had neither sufficient will nor the energy, time, or resources to take on a task as daunting as the remaking of the farm. But more consonant with the story here, they were also simply intimidated by the power and unshakable resolution brandished by the warring forces on the field. The trustees were also somewhat at fault, unwilling for many of the same reasons to dive back into the highly charged scene the farm had become. They were wooed away from the goal of continuing the mission of the farm, too, through the lure presented by the benefits of selling it. In their case, the role of the radical upstarts was played by the farm's new, younger residents.

In light of Epstein's observations, the moral contrasts of the farm's particular case can be, on close inspection, quite stark. Ambassadors of idealism subverting their own community. One, who tells us that leadership should be temporary, leading covertly for years. Another, who admonishes that losing the farm would be "an enormous detriment" to the community, conspiring himself to assist in bringing about its loss. The sad recognition that the farm no longer represented a beacon of hope, and the consequent prescription for action less palatable than merely effective. Advocates of peace and love—a number of them influenced by pacific Eastern religions—fighting each other tooth and nail. (By my own rough count, no fewer than ten lawyers were involved.) Notable accomplishments notwithstanding, this was, as John Wilton put it, "the price of our youthful dreams."

All of this would be little more than a coincidence if it didn't resonate far beyond a simple comparison of the Clamshell Alliance with the farm. In fact, as Epstein points out, and is clear to anyone who has studied the era of the 1960s or lived through it, such problems were the common fate of idealistic organizations throughout the period. In 1969, just as the farm was finding its footing, SDS (Students for a Democratic Society) had undergone a trauma very similar to the one that would later befall the Clamshell Alliance and then the farm. In the case of SDS, it led to the dubious career of the Weather Underground and the consequent loss of one of the largest and most hopeful political organizations then active in the United States. Earlier, the split in the Liberation News Service that had led to the founding of the farm had followed virtually the same course. The rift in MUSE later proceeded along a similar path. Many more examples could be found.

In all of these cases, I think we need to ask not only who won but also what has been lost. In the story of the farm, it seems to me that while

Harvey and Sam each saved face through the sale of the farm to the Peacemakers, neither of them really won. The community benefited only in that someone else was found to pursue the principles they espoused. For while the smoke and the haze of the battle and the relative success of its end tended to obscure it, the loss of the farm really represented the end of all in the physical realm that we in our idealism had managed to build together over a period of thirty-five years. Most of the hope and possible plans, except by way of our new surrogates the Peacemakers, had to be abandoned. No new way station, no vacation or study center, no farm retirement or joint investment plans, no garden retreat for our children, no joint extension of our shared political and social values into the coming years. It would be hard not to conclude that for our group itself, any possible next chapter in the social experiment that had been Montague Farm, a bellwether enterprise of its time, had ended in failure. For me, it stands as a monumental warning against the harmful role of arrogance, on the one hand, and the need, on the other, for idealistic communities and individuals, no matter how large or small—nation, town, or farm—to remain vigilant in the defense of their values. Looking around me, I would say that the time for this is always, and now.

Postscript

In the winter of 2010–2011, the farm was once again for sale. Again, concerned citizens of the larger community began meeting to look into its possible future. Unfortunately, the extensive renovations completed by the Zen Peacemakers, which made it unaffordable for them to keep, also made it unlikely that any of the former farm family could manage to repurchase the farm; its value was now almost fifty times the original price of the farm, the equivalent of one farm each for the fifty people who spent the most time there.

Dan Keller, one of Marshall's closest friends, has long been involved in the fate of the farm. At a farm-family gathering in the spring of 2011, we spoke of the situation as it was then, agreeing that, again, it would take a miracle to save the farm.

"Well," he said with the sort of resigned hope that age and experience have brought most of us, "if it leaves the family or the nonprofit world, it will simply be another chapter in the history of the property. If there's one thing we've learned," he mused, looking out at the many people congregated in a Vermont farmyard on a beautiful day in early May, "it's that the spirit is more important than the property."

As the gathered voices rose in one of the old songs we like to sing, I sensed that this was perhaps our way of finally declaring: Amen.

DRAMATIS PERSONAE

John Anderson. Husband of Susan Mareneck. The couple were early farm residents who soon moved to a nearby house of their own. John became a musician, luthier, and physician.

Marshall Bloom. Student radical, cofounder of Liberation News Service, founder of Montague Farm. Marshall took his own life on November 1, 1969, only a year after the founding of the farm.

Chuck and Nina. Survivors of a neighboring commune fire who arrived at the farm with the Chuckbus crew and stayed on for a number of years. Chuck is chief executive officer of Green Mountain Post films. Nina is an activist now based at Wendell Farm.

Clamshell Alliance. Regional anti-nuclear activist group with strong ties to Montague Farm.

Michael Curry (farm trustee). Early farm resident, college friend of fellow midwesterner Steve Marsden; later professor of geography at UCLA.

Steve Diamond (farm trustee). Early farm resident. Raised in Panama and Miami, he moved to Montague Farm with Liberation News Service and wrote *What the Trees Said* (1971), the first history of the farm. He later worked as a writer, social worker, and editor. Steve died in 2006.

Fellowship of Religious Youth (FRY; the trust). The group of seven trustees to whom Marshall left the farm on his death in 1969: Michael Curry, Steve Diamond, James Tapley (Lazarus Quon), Steve Marsden, Cathy Rogers, Harvey Wasserman, and John Wilton.

Friends of Montague Farm. Informal extended farm-family group organized to assist in discussions at farm's twenty-fifth anniversary gathering in 1993.

Bernie Glassman. Founder and *roshi* of the Zen Peacemakers, eventual buyers of the farm.

Green Mountain Post Films. Dan Keller and Chuck Light's independent film company, whose first film told the story of Sam Lovejoy and the proposed Montague nuclear plant.

Anna Gyorgy. Resident of the farm in its early years; later an anti-nuclear activist, editor, and global advocate for women's issues.

Irv and Greg. Early Montague residents with farming experience; college friends of Marshall Bloom and others in the farm family.

Janice and Sequoya Frey. Arrived at the farm with the Chuckbus crew after a fire at a neighboring commune and became long-term residents. Janice is a health care worker, Sequoya a designer. Janice's needs were central to ongoing discussions about the farm.

Marty Jezer. Antiwar and political activist, writer, longtime resident of nearby Packer Corners Farm in Guilford, Vermont.

Dan Keller. Founder and longtime resident of nearby Wendell Farm, close friend of Marshall Bloom, filmmaker, responsible neutral player in discussions over the future of the farm. Dan is founder and president of Green Mountain Post Films.

Lazarus Quon (James Tapley) (farm trustee). Young Floridian who moved to Montague Farm with Liberation News Service; later a master bookbinder and expert on Islamic art.

Tom Lesser. Neighbor and attorney who offered advice on the future of the farm.

Liberation News Service (LNS). The counterculture news service for the underground press founded by Ray Mungo and Marshall Bloom in 1967. Its offices were first in Washington, and then New York City. In August 1968 Marshall moved his portion of the news service from New York to Montague Farm.

Sam Lovejoy. Early farm resident, college friend of several in the farm's extended family; later an attorney and environmental and anti-nuclear activist. Sam was a central actor in farm debates.

Susan Mareneck. Early farm resident and wife of John Anderson; the couple soon moved to a nearby house of their own. Susan became a teacher, artist, and social advocate. Her group Friends of Montague Farm played a strong role in the farm's twenty-fifth reunion.

Eve Marko. Wife of Bernie Glassman; *sensei* and head of education for the Zen Peacemakers, eventual buyers of the farm.

Steve Marsden (farm trustee). Peace activist and student at New College, Florida, moved to Montague Farm with Liberation News Service; later returned to his native Iowa.

Tony Mathews. Early farm resident via the anti-war movement, often the farm's principal farmer; later a builder and cabinetmaker.

Montague Evergreen Foundation (MEF). New nonprofit organized in 2000 by Harvey Wasserman and others to promote their views on the future of Montague Farm.

Raymond Mungo. Student radical, co-founder of Liberation News Service, founder of Packer Corners Farm. In later life Raymond continued to be a writer and social critic, as well as a publisher, social worker, and advocate for gay rights.

Musicians United for Safe Energy (MUSE). National anti-nuclear activist group with strong ties to Montague Farm.

Peter Natti. Long-term resident of the farm, cabinetmaker, keeper of the farm's financial records during his tenure there.

Cathy Rogers (Cathy Hutchison) (farm trustee). Moved to Montague Farm with Steve Diamond and Liberation News Service, and initiated organic farming there. Cathy later became a naturopathic physician based in Seattle. (In the Documents section, Cathy is often referred to as Cathy Hutchison, her earlier married name.)

Smokey (Mark) Fuller and Judie Sloan. Arrived at the farm with the Chuckbus group after a neighboring commune fire; lived at the farm for a number of years. Smokey later became a builder, and Judie a writer.

Tim and Lise. Young organic farmers who spent nearly a decade at the farm.

Harvey Wasserman ("Sluggo") (farm trustee). Moved to Montague Farm with Liberation News Service; major protagonist in farm debates. Raised in

Ohio, where he eventually returned, Harvey is a longtime activist, writer, and journalist.

John Wilton (farm trustee). Moved to Montague Farm with Liberation News Service; later a photographer, graphic designer, and producer of classical Indian music based in New York.

Zen Peacemakers (Peacemaker Circle International, Bernie Glassman, Eve Marko). Buddhist group focusing on social activism, eventual buyers of the farm.

DOCUMENTS
ℭ
Memo from Marshall, 1969

Excerpt from a draft for a founding document for Montague Farm.

we are people who have travelld about a bit and now find ourselves here, where chaos stops at our border and Nature's order and unity may begin. In joining together by the compact below, and signing each one of us our own full names as if each were a unit distinct and whole apart from ourselves or the universe, we recognize that the event of a vote taken among us is a temporary falling from the organic grace which we seek, an expedient used merely to save ourselves for the future possibility of unity and trust regained. We hope those times when each must stand apart as a distinct unit and cast his vote, when the will of some may prevail over the will and understanding of a single person or a few, are rare times and not vestiged with any false claims of sanctimony, rather than mere base survival. For we are here to do our will, and Nature's will, and seek a special unity of our hearts, minds, bodies, homes, trees and river.

we are pretty boy floyd associates, banded together as outlaws and renegades against that which is said to be lawful in the eyes of some. Our standards are our own or those of all times; we dismiss the disunity, and unnatural world and laws of the society around us, with a pick of our nose. We are each of us independent sovereign states because we know and revere our dependence on others here and on Nature.

this charter is a piece of paper written to give accepted and unnatural legal form to our sharing and caring, mostly because the pressures on us from the outside may at times be so great that we must have a strong buttress to meet them.

MARSHALL'S WILL, 1969

ℭ

Nov.1, 1969

this is my last will and testament:

all my property be given to a trust, Fellowship of Religious Youth, the corporate directors of which are those who live on our shared property in Montague, namely: Cathy Hutchison, John Wilton, James Tapley, Harvey Wasserman, Steve Diamond, Steve Marsden, Michael Curry, and others they shall name; that the executors of this will and testament are Raymond Mungo of Guilford, Vt. and Daniel Keller of Wendell, Mass., that the exception to the above be such property in my second floor closet as Raymond chooses to dispose of personally,* and Max, an Irish Setter, who is first to be offered to my parents and failing that is to be given to Daniel Keller, and my "papers," such as they are, which are Verandah Porche's of Guilford, Vt. and Daniel Keller's to dispose of as they wish.

Failing all this, in the event the legality of this document is not accepted, and my property reverts to my parents, Sam S. Bloom and Lillian Bloom of Denver, Colorado, I charge them with executing the above provisions to the best of their ability.

My love to all, especially my parents, and to too many to name here who have given me joy and love; would that my life could have been more help to them; I am sorry about all this,

[Signed]
Marshall Bloom

*and for which purposes he shall be the first person to go through the closet

TRUST DOCUMENT, 1970

ℭ

FELLOWSHIP OF RELIGIOUS YOUTH REALTY TRUST

WE, CATHERINE HUTCHISON, JOHN WILTON, JAMES TAPLEY, HARVEY WASSERMAN, STEVEN DIAMOND, STEVEN MARSDEN, and MICHAEL CURRY, all of Montague, Franklin County, Massachusetts, do hereby declare that we hold all the land and any other property, real, personal or mixed, of whatever nature which may simultaneously with the execution of this instrument or at any time hereafter be conveyed to us to be held as trustees of the FELLOWSHIP Of RELIGIOUS YOUTH REALTY TRUST for the following purposes and upon the following trusts:

FIRST: To manage and maintain and improve the same and to invest and re-invest the property and proceeds of the trust.

SECOND: The said trustees whose term shall include their successors, shall hold all the said property, funds and assets, now or hereafter held or paid, to or transferred or conveyed to said trustees or successors, as trustees hereunder, for the benefit of the members of the FELLOWSHIP Of RELIGIOUS YOUTH, an association of individuals residing at the present time on a farm located in Montague, Massachusetts, the original and to date the only members of which Fellowship of Religious Youth are the said CATHERINE HUTCHISON, JOHN WILTON, JAMES TAPLEY, HARVEY WASSERMAN, STEVEN DIAMOND, STEVEN MARSDEN, and MICHAEL CURRY. Each such member of the FELLOWSHIP Of RELIGIOUS YOUTH shall be entitled to an equal beneficial interest in this trust. It is declared that current members of the FELLOWSHIP Of RELIGIOUS YOUTH may enlarge the number of members of said Fellowship by admitting new members by a three-fifths (3/5) vote of the current members, and that after such point additional new members may be admitted to membership in the said Fellowship by a three-fifths (3/5) vote of all members of the said Fellowship at the time such vote is taken. No person shall be a member who has not reached his twentieth year of age. All new members shall have the same right as members of longer standing with respect to voting, and each new member shall be entitled to beneficial interest of each member of longer standing, such that at all times each member of the said Fellowship possesses a beneficial interest equal to that of every other member of said Fellowship. A member of said Fellowship shall continue to be a member in good standing unless said member either ceases living with the other members of the said Fellowship at the Fellowship's farm located in Montague, Massachusetts, or any other locus or loci where the Fellowship resides or where the trustees acquire property for the benefit of said Fellowship, or unless said member is deprived of membership by a four-fifths (4/5) vote of the members of said Fellowship at the time such vote is taken. However, it is expressly recognized, understood and agreed that from time to time certain members of the Community will be engaged in activities which will necessitate their absenting themselves from physical presence on property of the Fellowship, and such members shall not be automatically deprived of membership under this paragraph provided that their absence is approved by a majority of the Trustees. All elections hereunder shall be conducted and recorded by a person or persons appointed for such purpose by the trustees hereunder. It is hereby expressly declared that a Trust and not a partnership is hereby created; that neither the trustees nor the beneficiaries or either or any of them shall ever be personally liable hereunder as partners or otherwise be required to see to the application of any monies or other considerations paid by said trustees, but that for all acts and liabilities, if any, the trustees only shall be liable as such, and then to the extent of the trust fund only. Nothing herein shall be construed as restricting the locus of said Fellowship to said Montague, and the Fellowship may even occupy more than one locus at a time.

THIRD: To collect and receive the income thereof, to pay all expenses thereof with full and conclusive power to determine what shall be charged against income and what against principal. It is expressly provided that the trustees shall be privileged to share all costs of such improvements or alterations of the property or any part thereof against income.

FOURTH: To pay to the beneficiaries the net income or such portion as the trustees shall deem advisable.

FIFTH: The trustees shall have and exercise all the power of an owner of any and all property held from time to time hereunder. The trustees are authorized and empowered to sell, transfer, or convey free from trust any part or all of the trust property; to mortgage any part or the whole of said premises and to sign, execute, seal and deliver such mortgages and negotiable instruments; to let or lease any part of all of the trust property even for terms which might exceed the term of this trust.

SIXTH: No mortgagee or purchaser from the trustees shall be bound to see to the application of any money or thing of value paid to the trustees.

SEVENTH: Any trustee may resign this trust by written instrument executed by him and recorded with the Registry of Deeds for the County of Franklin in the Commonwealth of Massachusetts. In the event of resignation, death or other incapacity of a trustee to act, a successor trustee shall be appointed by a majority of the remaining trustees hereunder, and any successor trustee shall be deemed duly qualified upon the recording in the Registry of Deeds for the county of Franklin in the Commonwealth of Massachusetts of a document appointing him, duly executed by the majority of the remaining trustees, with his acceptance of the trust endorsed thereon.

EIGHTH: The trustees shall have no power to bind the beneficiaries personally, and no person having any claim against the trust shall have the right to look beyond the trust property, and no beneficiary hereunder shall have any interest in the trust property subject to alienation, anticipation or the claim of any creditor.

NINTH: The trustees shall be liable only for their own willful misconduct, and shall specifically incur no personal liability with respect to any matter that shall call for an exercise of judgment.

TENTH: Holders of four-fifths (4/5) of the beneficial interest may at any time alter, amend or modify this trust by the recording with the Registry of Deeds for the County of Franklin in the Commonwealth of Massachusetts of an instrument executed and sealed by said holders of majority of the beneficial interest, setting forth such alteration, amendment or modification.

ELEVENTH: This trust shall terminate on February 1, 1980, or at an earlier date by a two-thirds (2/3) vote of the then trustees, recorded with the Registry of Deeds for the County of Franklin.

TWELFTH: Upon termination of this trust, the trustees shall after payment of all charges and expenses divide the net proceeds among all of the then beneficiaries of the said trust.

THIRTEENTH: All moneys or capital outlays that are expended by the trustees to fulfill their trusts as aforementioned must be agreed upon by three-fifths (3/5) of the trustees or their successors in order to bind the trust, unless said moneys or capital outlay does not exceed Two Hundred ($200) Dollars, or an emergency situation arises where there is not sufficient time to contact the fellow trustees for approval of an expenditure designed to protect the beneficiaries from loss exceeding the amount expended.

FOURTEENTH: The beneficial interests in the trust are not transferable or assignable and are for the sole use and enjoyment of the beneficiaries who become beneficiaries by virtue of their admission into membership in the said FELLOWSHIP Of RELIGIOUS YOUTH. As such, a beneficiary hereunder ceases to be such if and when he or she ceases to be a member or leaves the said Fellowship as provided in Paragraph SECOND above, and such beneficiary shall not be entitled to any compensation or share of the trust assets upon ceasing to be a member and beneficiary hereunder.

FIFTEENTH: It is expressly declared that the Trust assets hereunder are to be managed with a principal purpose of maintaining the cohesion and continuation of the FELLOWSHIP OF RELIGIOUS YOUTH, and with a secondary purpose of providing sufficient income to maintain the properties held by the trust, and with tertiary purpose of making a profit.

Signed and sealed this _____ day of _____ , A.D. 1970.

_____.

THE COMPLAINT, 2000

ℭ

COMMONWEALTH OF MASSACHUSETTS
TRIAL COURT

FRANKLIN, SS
LAND COURT DEPARTMENT
MISC. CASE NO. 268070

MONTAGUE EVERGREEN FOUNDATION, INC., PLAINTIFF

vs.

|AMES TAPLEY, |OHN WILTON, MICHAEL CURRY, STEPHEN DIAMOND,

CATHY HUTCHISON, SAMUEL LOVE|OY, |ANICE FREY, HARVEY WASSERMAN,

STEVEN MARSDEN, individually and as they are or claim to be Trustees of the

Fellowship of Religious Youth Realty Trust, Defendants

COMPLAINT

Introduction

NOTE: This introduction is for information purposes only: it does not require a responsive pleading by any defendant.

This case involves ownership of the Montague Farm (the "farm") in Montague, Massachusetts. A previous owner, Marshall Irving Bloom, wanted the farm to be a nonprofit organization, serving the higher goals of peace, human harmony and organic living. The farm passed from Marshall's estate to a realty trust set up to serve those purposes. The purpose of this lawsuit is to fulfill that original intent by keeping ownership of the farm in a nonprofit organization.

As the sole remaining beneficiary when the realty trust expired, Harvey Wasserman conveyed the farm to the Montague Evergreen Foundation, Inc., a nonprofit corporation established for the express purpose of carrying out the original mandate of Montague Farm and its founder.

In 1988, money for the purchase of Montague Farm came from a benefit showing of a Beatles film ("Magical Mystery Tour") whose proceeds went to further the work of the Liberation New Service, which Marshall Bloom helped found and direct. Marshall used part of those funds to move part of the news service to western Massachusetts. Over time, a strong community grew up at the Montague Farm, with a continual flow of committed people that remains to this day.

When Marshal Bloom died in November, 1969, he left the farm in the stewardship of a realty trust, naming seven trustees and beneficiaries. A trust document was recorded the following year and a deed was recorded in 1973, both in the local registry of deeds. When the trust expired by its own terms in 1980, Harvey Wasserman was the only trustee and beneficiary remaining in residence at the farm. He then became the sole owner of the Montague Farm (note 1).

Over the decades, the fluid community that has thrived in and around Montague Farm has repeatedly confirmed its commitment never to sell this unique treasure. While there have been disagreements over the years, no one has ever been formally evicted. In 1993, a large gathering of many of those who have lived there over the years reaffirmed Marshall Bloom's original communal vision and vowed that the farm should continue to be a place where that vision could be realized.

Today, Montague Farm is a vibrant, functioning community center. The property is well maintained and well utilized. Seven adults now live there with two children who were born there (another child is on the way). Of those adults, two have been in residence for about eight years, one for six years and two have lived there for five years.

Montague Farm remains, in essence, a living fulfillment of the original intent of its founder, Marshall Bloom, and of those who provided that original down payment in support of the Liberation News Service.

In June of 2000, farm residents and the remaining beneficiary (Harvey Wasserman) formed a non-profit organization, Montague Evergreen Foundation, Inc., to continue this cooperative living and working arrangement while preserving intact an operating organic farm.

The articles of organization of the Montague Evergreen Foundation require that the farm cannot be sold, except to another nonprofit organization (and then only under extreme circumstances) with no individual receiving any profit from the sale.

Sadly, some original trustees and former residents have challenged the original vision, speaking of a private sale from which they would profit individually, and even raising the prospect of forcible evictions. This would be an abandonment of Marshall Bloom's vision, confirmed over the years by the larger Montague Farm community, of a better world in which people work together cooperatively for the common good.

This action is filed in the hopes of keeping that vision a living reality at Montague Farm for generations to come.

(note 1) Harvey Wassermann became aware of his status as sole beneficiary in the summer of 1999, when other original trustees began pressing for sale of Montague Farm. The other original trustees left Montague Farm in the years following Marshall Bloom's death, and played little or no role in the farm's operation. Wasserman (who was a high school friend of Bloom and a co-founder of Liberation News Service) remained in residence at the Farm though the early 1980's. In the ensuing years, he continued to play a vital role at Montague Farm; visiting frequently, establishing personal relationships with new residents, signing on to the farm's insurance policy, and making interest free loans to fund farm improvements. He has forsworn any personal financial gain from the farm, and respectfully disagrees with those original trustees who want the farm to be sold off for their own personal profit.

Parties

NOTE: All recorded documents referred to in this complaint are recorded in the Franklin County Registry of Deeds in Greenfield.

I   Plaintiff Montague Evergreen Foundation, Inc. (herein "Montague Evergreen Foundation") is a duly organized and existing Massachusetts nonprofit corporation, with its principal office at 177 Ripley Road, Montague, Franklin County, Massachusetts 01351.

2.   Defendants are natural persons whose names and addresses are as follows:

    a. James Tapley, [address]

    b. John Wilton, [address]

    c. Michael Curry, [address]

    d. Stephen Diamond, also known as Steven Diamond, [address]

    e. Cathy Hutchison, now know as Cathy Rogers, [address]

    f. Samuel Lovejoy, [address]

    g. Janice Frey, [address]

    h. Steven Marsden, [address]

    i. Harvey Wasserman, [address]

3.   This case concerns the title to real estate commonly known (and hereafter referred to) as the Montague Farm, whose address is 177 Ripley Road, Montague, Massachusetts; the Montague Farm was formerly owned by the late Marshal Irving Bloom whose estate is Franklin County Probate # 43688.

4.   By deed dated November 23, 1973, recorded at Book 1372, Page 326, Stephen A. Diamond, as Administrator of the estate of Marshall Irving Bloom, conveyed the Montague Farm to a grantee described as follows: "Fellowship of Religious Youth Realty Trust, a Massachusetts Realty Trust created by an instrument on September 22, 1970 and recorded in Franklin County Registry of Deeds, Book 1266, Page 446" (hereafter called the "trust instrument").

5.   The Fellowship of Religious Youth Realty Trust was a Massachusetts Realty Trust (hereafter called "the trust") created by an instrument on September 22, 1970 and recorded in Franklin County Registry of Deeds, Book 1266, Page 445.

6.   The second paragraph of the trust instrument stated that the trust was "to benefit the members of the Fellowship of Religious Youth, an association of individuals residing at the present time [e.g. in September of 1970] [*sic*] on a farm located in Montague, Massachusetts, the original and to date the only members of which Fellowship of Religious Youth are the said Cathy Hutchison, John Wilton, James Tapley, Harvey Wasserman, Steven Diamond, Steven Marsden, and Michael Curry."

7.   The Eleventh paragraph of the trust instrument states: "This trust shall terminate on February 1, 1980, or at an earlier date by two-thirds vote of the then trustees recorded with the Registry of Deeds for the County of Franklin."

8.   The Second paragraph of the trust instrument states in part that "A member of said Fellowship shall continue to be a member in good standing unless said member

either ceases living with the other members of the said Fellowship at the Fellowship's farm located in Montague, Massachusetts, or any other locus or loci where the Fellowship resides or where the trustees acquire property for the benefit of said Fellowship, or unless said member is deprived of membership by a four-fifths (4/5) vote of the members of said Fellowship."

9.　(a) When the trust terminated on February I, 1980, the only remaining beneficiary was defendant Harvey Wasserman

　　　(b) By operation of law, when the trust instrument terminated on February I, 1980 pursuant to the Eleventh paragraph of the trust instrument, ownership of the Montague Farm devolved on defendant Harvey Wasserman as the then remaining sole beneficiary of the trust.

10.　Defendant Harvey Wasserman conveyed the Montague Farm, whose address is 177 Ripley Road, Montague, Massachusetts, to the plaintiff Montague Evergreen Foundation by a deed dated June 27, 2000, recorded at Book 3643, Page 118.

11. The Tenth paragraph of the trust instrument states: "Holders of four-fifths (4/5) of the beneficial interest may at any time alter, amend, or modify this trust by the recording with the Registry of Deeds for the County of Franklin in the Commonwealth of Massachusetts of an instrument executed and sealed by said holders of a majority of the beneficial interest, setting forth such alteration, amendment, or modification."

12.　There was a purported "Alteration, Amendment and Modification of Trust Entitled Fellowship of Religious Youth Realty Trust" (hereafter called "the purported trust amendment") dated August 11, 1979, and recorded January 24, 1983 at Book 1717, Page 122.

13.　Notwithstanding the date of August 11, 1979, the purported trust amendment was not actually signed on that date, but was signed after February I, 1980, by the persons whose signatures appear thereon.

14.　No "alteration, amendment or modification" of the trust was recorded in the Franklin County Registry of Deeds prior to the termination of the trust on February I, 1980.

15.　The purported trust amendment was not recorded until nearly three years after the termination of the trust.

16　Following the recording of the purported trust amendment, no deed was ever executed and recorded conveying the Montague Farm back to the purportedly amended trust.

17.　(a) The trust instrument named defendants Cathy Hutchison (now known as Cathy Rogers), John Wilton, James Tapley, Stephen Diamond (also known as Steven Diamond), Steven Marsden, Harvey Wasserman and Michael Curry, "as trustees of the Fellowship of Religious Youth Realty Trust."

　　　(b) Defendant Janice Frey claims: (i) that she was named a trustee (and also a beneficiary) of the trust at a meeting of the trustees held on August 11, 1993; and (ii) that she has been an "Acting Trustee" of the trust since about 1975.

(c) Defendant Samuel Lovejoy is a former resident of the Montague Farm who on information and belief claims an ownership interest therein, and may also claim to have the status of trustee *de facto* if not *de jure.*

18. (a) Defendant Frey has seized and occupied as a dwelling an outbuilding on the Montague Farm since about 1994.

(b) Defendant Frey submitted to the Town of Montague Zoning Board of Appeals an application for variance (Docket # 00-13, application dated May 17, 2000) that would have allowed defendant Frey to convert said outbuilding into a dwelling.

(c) After questions were raised concerning whether defendant Frey had the requisite ownership interest to proceed with her variance application, the public hearing on the application was continued and the application was subsequently withdrawn.

First Claim for Relief:
Action to Recover Freehold Estate (Writ of Entry, G.L. c. 237)

19. Plaintiff Montague Evergreen Foundation re-alleges paragraphs 1 through 18 above, as though fully set forth herein.

20. Defendant Frey has disseized plaintiff Montague Evergreen Foundation from possession of certain land or of certain buildings thereon, adversely to the title of the plaintiff.

21. Plaintiff Montague Evergreen Foundation has the right of entry and of full possession and enjoyment of the Montague Farm.

22. Defendant Frey has wrongfully deprived the plaintiff Montague Evergreen Foundation of its right of entry of possession of a portion of the Montague Farm.

23. The land Court has exclusive original jurisdiction of this action pursuant to G.L. c. 185 §1(c).

WHEREFORE, plaintiff Montague Evergreen Foundation prays that this honorable Court: issue to it a writ of seisin against defendant Frey, and order said defendant to vacate said land and building(s) forthwith; award plaintiff Montague Evergreen Foundation the costs of this action; and grant such other and further relief as the Court deems just.

Second Claim for Relief:
Petition to Compel Adverse Claimant to Try Title
G.L. c.240 §§ 1–5

24. Plaintiff Montague Evergreen Foundation re-alleges paragraphs 1 through 23 above, as though fully set forth herein.

25. (a) Defendant Janice Frey has clouded the title to the Montague Farm by seizing an outbuilding thereon and asserting an ownership interest therein. .

(b) On information and belief, defendant Samuel Lovejoy has clouded the title to the Montague Farm by asserting an ownership interest therein.

26.   One of more of the defendants have clouded the title to the Montague Farm by an adverse claim, by asserting that they are or will be on February 1, 2001 (the expiration date of the purported trust amendment) owners of the Montague Farm as tenants in common. Said defendants further assert that as tenants in common they have the right and standing to bring an action for partition of the Montague Farm.

27.   The Land Court has exclusive original jurisdiction of this action pursuant to G.L. c. 185 § 1(d).

WHEREFORE, plaintiff Montague Evergreen Foundation prays that this honorable Court: adjudicate the adverse claims to the disputed land and title thereto; determine that no defendant has any right or standing to bring an action for partition of the Montague Farm; award plaintiff the costs of this action; and grant such other and further relief as the Court deems just.

Third Claim for Relief:
Suit in Equity to Quiet Title, G.L. c. 240, §§ 6–10

28.   Plaintiff Montague Evergreen Foundation re-alleges paragraphs 1 through 26 above, as though fully set forth herein.

29.   The Land Court has jurisdiction of this action pursuant to G.L. c. 240 § 6.

WHEREFORE, plaintiff Montague Evergreen Foundation prays that this honorable Court: adjudicate the adverse claims to the disputed land and title thereto; determine that no defendant has any right to bring an action for partition of the Montague Farm; award plaintiff the costs of this action; and grant such other and further relief as the Court deems just.

Fourth Claim for Relief:
Declaratory Judgment, G.L. c 231

30.   Plaintiff Montague Evergreen Foundation re-alleges paragraphs 1 though 26 above, as though fully set forth herein.

31.   There exists between the parties to this action an actual justifiable controversy within the jurisdiction of this court concerning:

a. Ownership of the Montague Farm by plaintiff Montague Evergreen Foundation;

b. Whether defendant Frey has any right to occupy or possess any part of the Montague Farm;

c. Whether defendants are or will be on February 1, 2001 (the expiration date of the purported trust amendment) owners of the Montague Farms as tenants in common

d. Whether defendants have any right or standing to bring an action for partition of the Montague Farm.

32.   The Land Court has jurisdiction of this action pursuant to G.L. c. 231A, § 1.

WHEREFORE, plaintiff Montague Evergreen Foundation prays that this honorable Court: adjudicate the adverse claims to the disputed land and title thereto; determine that no defendant has any right to bring an action for partition of the Montague Farm; award plaintiff the costs of this action; and grant such other and further relief as the Court deems just.

Fifth Claim for Relief
Declaratory Judgment, G.L. c. 231

33.   Plaintiff Montague Evergreen Foundation re-alleges paragraphs 1 through 18 above, as though fully set forth herein.

34.   The natural persons who now occupy the Montague Farm (some of whom have occupied the premises for several years), claim the status of life tenants, based on an oral agreement with the defendants which they have performed by occupying the Montague Farm, paying taxes, insurance and utilities thereon, and by repairing and maintaining the premises, all without financial support from the defendants (other than defendant Harvey Wasserman).

35.   Said occupants have assigned or are in the process of assigning all right, title and interest they may have in the Montague Farm to the plaintiff Montague Evergreen Foundation.

36.   There exists between the parties to this action an actual justifiable controversy within the jurisdiction of this court concerning whether the plaintiff Montague Evergreen Foundation as assignee of the current occupants has the status of life tenant for the lives of those occupants.

37.   The Land Court has jurisdiction of this action pursuant to G.L. c. 231A, § 1.

WHEREFORE, plaintiff Montague Evergreen Foundation prays that this honorable Court: adjudicate the adverse claims to the disputed land and title thereto; determine that the plaintiff Montague Evergreen Foundation as assignee of the current occupants has the status of life tenant for the lives of those occupants; award plaintiff the costs of this action; and grant such other and further relief as the Court deems just.

Plaintiff Montague Evergreen Foundation, by its attorney,

_____, Esq.   Dated: December 1, 2000

[Address]

NOTES

❦

1. ORIGINS (1968)

5. *affluent society:* See Galbraith, *The Affluent Society.* Another informative view of the role of the 1950s in the development of the 1960s is Payne, "Roll Over, Norman Rockwell." See also Jezer, *The Dark Ages.*

5. *a great shock to professor Kerr:* Clark Kerr, an economist and professor of industrial relations, was the first chancellor of the University of California, Berkeley (1952–1957), and later president of the entire UC system (1958–1967). His handling of Berkeley's Free Speech Movement in the mid-1960s brought him criticism from all sides of the institution he is widely credited with building. As a result, he became the iconic representative of the large-scale, impersonal education strongly disliked by the radical youth of the time.

6. *The late years of the decade:* For an overview of the entire period, see Gitlin, *The Sixties.*

6. *Kerner Report:* Kerner, *Report of the National Advisory Commission on Civil Disorders.*

8. *Liberation News Service:* In addition to Mungo's *Famous Long Ago*, a more recent treatment of LNS and its significance in the underground press movement, including a number of observations relevant to the later farm story, is McMillian, *Smoking Typewriters.*

8. *the conventional student press network:* In the months leading up to the founding of LNS, Mungo and Bloom had been preparing to lead the United States Student Press Association, a national organization of student newspaper editors, located in Washington, DC.

9. *the movement:* This word, so central to the ethos of the time, is sometimes capitalized in writing on the 1960s.

12. *While it didn't always prove to be:* For more on the author's views on such matters see Fels, *Farm Friends.*

13. *The move was complete:* See Lerner, "The Liberation of the Liberation News Service."

2. EARLY DAYS (1968–1969)

15–16. *chaos and disorganization . . . we had to suffer the fickleness of random energy:* Diamond, *What the Trees Said,* 38.

16. *Yippie-run In-hog-uration:* This satirical un-celebration of the Nixon inauguration, featuring a live pig, was advertised to run from January 18–20, 1969. For a detailed and fascinating report on this event, see "Rights in Concord: The Response to the Counter-Inaugural Protest Activities in Washington, D.C., January 18–20, 1969," prepared by the Task Force on Law and Law Enforcement for the National Commission on the Causes and Prevention of Violence, available at www.archive.org. The In-hog-uration is covered on pp. 80–81 and 93–94.

17. *to regain the meager comforts:* From the opening of Bierce's short story "The Boarded Window."

20. *With books like. . . :* Popular works included Richard Brautigan's *Trout Fishing in America* (1967) and *In Watermelon Sugar* (1968); Kurt Vonnegut's *Cat's Cradle* (1963); and Hermann Hesse's *Demian, Steppenwolf,* and *Siddhartha* (all first published between 1919 and 1927 but newly popular in translation throughout the 1960s). For the even more mystically inclined there was Mikhail Bulgakov's *The Master and Margarita* (first available in English in 1967).

3. FARM LIFE (1969–1973)

26. *"The New Peasantry":* Rodale, "Young People—Are They America's New Peasantry?"

27. *an offshoot of the farm:* On Irv's farming experiment in Willet, New York, see Plimpton, *1975 Farm Journal.*

28. *Venceremos Brigade:* This organization is still active. As noted on its website (www.venceremosbrigade.net/), "In 1969, a coalition of young people formed the Venceremos ('We Shall Overcome') Brigade, as a means of showing solidarity with the Cuban Revolution by working side by side with Cuban workers and challenging U.S. policies towards Cuba."

29. *he completed work on a book:* Wasserman, *Harvey Wasserman's History of the United States.*

30. *The shock of Marshall's death:* At the time, Bloom's suicide was noted and commented upon widely. More than three years later, in the spring of 1973, a young David Eisenhower, who had known Bloom briefly at Amherst College, was still using him as a foil to discuss, in a national op–ed piece titled "In Memory of Campus Activism," what he saw as the final demise of the era of student revolt.

The strong published responses of several of Bloom's colleagues from that time suggest that Eisenhower's assessment was incorrect; see Nathan and Blum, "Some Other Memories of Marshall Bloom," and Coburn, "Why Marshall Bloom Died." For further study see Goldberg, "Tragic, Magic Marshall"; Stevens, *Daniel Shays' Legacy?*; and Slonecker, "We Are Marshall Bloom." Marshall's death is also dealt with at length by Steve Diamond in *What the Trees Said.*

4. RENEWED ACTIVISM (1974–1982)

33. *an essay he wrote:* Lovejoy, "Somebody's Got to Do It."
34. *Sam's statement:* A condensed version of Sam's tower statement appears in Wasserman's *Energy War,* 29–30.
36. *grassroots antinuclear movement:* For a thorough account of antinuclear activity in western Massachusetts at this time see Surbrug, *Beyond Vietnam.*
38. *As a regional umbrella organization:* For an overview of the Clamshell Alliance and its larger context see Epstein, *Political Protest and Cultural Revolution,* 58–91. For a firsthand account, see Wasserman, *Energy War,* 27–129.
44. *largest set of events ever:* The MUSE concerts are reported in McLane, "MUSE: Rock Politics Comes of Age."

5. NEW DIRECTIONS (1983–1992)

47. *concerts, . . . records, . . . feature film:* For the output of MUSE, see the bibliography.
48. *an activist organization of her own:* Anna's organization is Women and Life on Earth, www.wloe.org/ .
51. *I loved writing the book:* This and other recent material on Harvey Wasserman are from the author's interview with him, July 2006.
53. *George from Wendell Farm:* George D. Sherman, anthropologist and author of *Rice, Rupees, and Ritual: Economy and Society among the Samosir Batak of Sumatra* (1990).
56. *an interview in 2008:* Except where noted, all quotes from Sam Lovejoy in this section are from an interview conducted by Blake Slonecker for his dissertation, "Living the Movement." I am indebted to Blake Slonecker for providing me with a full transcript of this interview.
59. *related to Elijah Lovejoy:* The similarity between these two historic Lovejoys is striking, including the central role for each of a printing press. Elijah's brother Owen, a close friend of Abraham Lincoln, is also a historical figure of considerable interest.
59. *a much earlier interview:* Author interview with Sam Lovejoy, 1980.
61. *back in his MUSE days:* Author interview with Sam Lovejoy, 1980.
61. *I'd fallen in love:* Diamond, "Sam Lovejoy's Nuclear War," 36.
63. *she recalled not long ago:* Author conversation with Janice Frey, 2006.
66. *I went to see him at his home:* Author interview with Peter Natti, 2006.

6. THE REUNION (1993)

78. *left the farm to a trust:* The text of Marshall's will is included in the Documents section at the back of this book.

79. *this document:* For the text of the realty trust, see the Documents section.

82. *Friends of Montague Farm:* The account here of the Friends and the farm reunion, including quotations, is largely derived from materials in the personal collections of several farm family members, as well as the author's own recollections.

7. AFTERMATH (1994–1999)

96. *pointed out to me:* Author interview with Peter Natti, 2006.

8. ANNUS HORRIBILIS (2000)

100. *Cathy asked Harvey:* The overall discussion of the farm's future here is distilled largely from farm family e-mails of the time.

101. *in his correspondence:* As capitalization and other matters of style are often considered a matter of personal expression among the farm family and its generation, direct quotes from correspondence in this book are left as much as possible in their original form.

104. *characteristic, if quirky, document:* This memo from Marshall is included in the Documents section at the back of this book.

106. *just regular people:* Diamond, *What the Trees Said,* 51–52.

108. *public transgressions in the name of the New Age:* Bhagwan Shree Rajneesh was an Indian mystic whose Oregon sect was later involved in scandals of sex, money and crime; Jim Jones was American guru responsible for the suicide deaths of more than nine hundred of his followers in Guyana in 1978.

111. *We have until February:* From farm family e-mail correspondence, 2000.

111. *master bookbinder and expert on Islamic art:* In June 2006, for example, Tapley won the prestigious DeGolyer Triennial Award for American Bookbinding of the Bridwell Library, Southern Methodist University, Dallas, Texas.

122. *The third section:* This section is unfinished, but from a later iteration sent out in October, about a month later, and quoted here, its practical implications are clear.

123. *our locus:* Diamond's use of the word here is also a reference to this particular term, which was part of the discussion of the trustees' geographical location in relation to their continuing role in the trust.

129. *We believe that Montague Farm:* From farm family e-mails, 2000.

129. *a complaint of some ten pages:* The text of the complaint is included in the Documents section.

132. *As the official administrator:* Though not mentioned as such in Marshall's will, Steve Diamond, as one of his close associates, had later been appointed by Marshall's father as the administrator of his estate.

135. *just the sort of novel:* Besides *What the Trees Said,* his book on the farm, Steve

Diamond had also published the complex, New Age–influenced adventure novel *Panama Red* (1979), to which Janice is clearly referring here.

9. ANNUS LUCTUS (2001)

139. *Annus Luctus:* In Roman law and tradition, a year of mourning and waiting.

10. ANNUS MIRABILIS (2002)

150. *in an interview in 2006:* Author's interview with Harvey Wasserman, July 2006.
151. *Bonnie Raitt:* Award-winning musician, devoted political activist, founder and board member of MUSE.
152. *the scope and ambitiousness of their work:* Among Glassman's best known projects is the Greyston Bakery, in Yonkers, New York, founded in 1982. The proceeds from this highly successful business, run largely by the homeless, helped to fund the transformation of condemned and aging buildings into new housing for the poor. In 1991, Glassman received a Best of America Award for Social Action from *U.S. News & World Report.* The Peacemakers, founded in 1996, have become known for their many "street retreats" in which participants eat in soup kitchens and sleep in homeless shelters or public spaces and "Zazen takes place in parks and dokusan in alleys." See also Queen, *Engaged Buddhism in the West.*
154. *Montague Peace:* Steve Diamond, farm family e-mails, 2002.

11. THE FARM AND ITS LEGACY (2002–2006)

169. *website of its own:* http://zenpeacemakers.org/.
173. *The moment Steve had described:* Diamond, *What the Trees Said,* 6–7.
173. *"Kurt Vonnegut's concept of the* karass*":* A concept of extended family introduced by Kurt Vonnegut in his popular novel *Cat's Cradle.* The Urban Dictionary (www. urbandictionary.com) offers this concise and accurate definition: "A group of people linked in a cosmically significant manner, even when superficial linkages are not evident."
177. *The trickster of anthropology and myth:* For a more recent treatment of this subject see Hyde, *Trickster Makes This World.*
177. *what Campbell calls "a transcendent anonymity":* All quotations and summaries in this and the following paragraphs are from Campbell, *Hero with a Thousand Faces:* Edshu and transcendent anonymity, 44–46; Raven, 90, 207–9, 247–48; Maui, 182–85, 327; and passim.
180. *Epstein makes several points:* All quotations in the following section are from Epstein, *Political Protest and Cultural Revolution,* chapter 2.
183. *the common fate of idealistic organizations:* For a recent memoir of a counterculture farm with striking echoes to the story of Montague, see Coleman, *This Life Is in Your Hands.* See also Fels, "Troubled Prophet."

BIBLIOGRAPHY

Ɛ

Buying the Farm is one of a series of books about Montague Farm and its extended family, and part of a much larger number of books, articles, and other materials relating to the farm family on a wider scale. In *Famous Long Ago* Raymond Mungo tells the story of the Liberation News Service, and thus the ancient history, so to speak, of the Montague and Packer Corners farms. Mungo continues his narrative of early farm life, especially at Packer Corners, in his second book, *Total Loss Farm.* The story of Montague Farm's first year is to be found in Steve Diamond's *What the Trees Said. Buying the Farm* brings the Montague story up to date.

The larger bibliography related to *Buying the Farm* also includes many books by farm family authors. Some of particular relevance to the early days of the farm and its background are Marty Jezer's *The Dark Ages,* Asa Elliot's *The Bloom High Way,* Peter Gould's *Burnt Toast,* Stephen Davis's *Say Kids, What Time Is It?,* and Richard Wizansky's *Home Comfort.* Ray Mungo's *Beyond the Revolution* continues the story of farm family radicals in later days, as does my earlier book, *Farm Friends,* which contains the most thorough bibliography of the farm group to date. Further visual images of farm life can be found in Peter Simon's photographic collections *Moving On / Holding Still* and *I and Eye,* as well as in some of the works of Green Mountain Post Films.

Bothmer, Bernard von. *Framing the Sixties: The Use and Abuse of a Decade from Ronald Reagan to George W. Bush.* Amherst: University of Massachusetts Press, 2010.

Campbell, Joseph. *The Hero with a Thousand Faces.* 1949; repr., Cleveland: World Publishing, 1956.

Coburn, Judith. "Why Marshall Bloom Died" (letter to the editor). *New York Times,* May 30, 1973.

Coleman, Melissa. *This Life Is in Your Hands.* New York: HarperCollins, 2011.

Curry, Michael. *The Work in the World: Geographical Practice and the Written Word.* Minneapolis: University of Minnesota Press, 1996.

———. *Digital Places: Living with Geographic Information Technologies.* London: Routledge, 1998.

Davis, Stephen: *Say Kids! What Time Is It? Notes from the Peanut Gallery.* Boston: Little, Brown, 1987.

Diamond, Steve. *What the Trees Said.* New York: Delacorte Press, 1971; rev. ed., Center Ossipee, NH: Beech River Books, 2006.

———. "Sam Lovejoy's Nuclear War." *New Times,* October 1974, 30–36.

———. *Panama Red.* New York: Avon Books, 1979.

———. "Back to the Land." In Smith and Koster, *Time It Was,* 235–46.

Duberman, Martin. *Black Mountain: An Exploration in Community.* New York: E. P. Dutton, 1972.

Eisenhower, David. "In Memory of Campus Activism." *New York Times,* April 30, 1973.

Elliot, Asa. *The Bloom High Way.* New York: Delacorte Press, 1972.

Epstein, Barbara. *Political Protest and Cultural Revolution: Nonviolent Direct Action in the 1970s and 1980s.* Berkeley: University of California Press, 1991.

Fels, Tom., ed. *Farm Notes* (Montague Farm newsletter). Winter 1994

———. "Troubled Prophet: The Life and Death of Michael Metelica." *The Mind's Eye,* Spring 2006, 5–39.

———. *Farm Friends: From the Late Sixties to the West Seventies and Beyond.* North Bennington, VT: RSI, 2008.

———. "War Correspondents: The Story of Two Vietnam-era Classmates and Friends." *Amherst,* Fall 2009, 22–27.

Galbraith, Kenneth. *The Affluent Society.* Boston: Houghton Mifflin, 1958.

Gitlin, Todd. *The Sixties: Years of Hope, Days of Rage.* New York: Bantam, 1987.

Goldberg, Hillel. "Tragic, Magic Marshall: The Anatomy of a Suicide."
    Intermountain Jewish News, May 1986, 1–15.
Gould, Peter. *Burnt Toast.* New York: Alfred A. Knopf, 1972.
Green Mountain Post (first issue: *New Babylon Times;* sixth issue: *Farm
    Notes*), various authors, Montague, MA, 1969–1993. Green Moun-
    tain Post Films Records (MS 516), Special Collections and Uni-
    versity Archives, University of Massachusetts Amherst Libraries.
Green Mountain Post Films. Daniel Keller and Charles Light, producers
    and directors. (Several of these projects were done in conjunction
    with Steve Diamond, John Wilton, and others of the extended
    farm family.) *Lovejoy's Nuclear War*, 1975.
———. *Voices of Spirit*, 1975.
———. *Radiation and Health*, 1976.
———. *Training for Non-violence*, 1977.
———. *The Last Resort*, 1978.
———. *Save the Planet*, 1979.
———. *Vietnam: The Secret Agent*, 1983.
———. *Cannabis Rising*, 1996.
———. *Peace Trip*, 2000.
Gyorgy, Anna. *No Nukes: Everyone's Guide to Nuclear Power.* Boston: South
    End Press, 1979.
Hyde, Lewis. *Trickster Makes This World.* New York: North Point Press, 1998.
Jezer, Marty. *The Dark Ages: Life in the United States, 1945–1960.* Boston:
    South End Press, 1982.
Kerner, Otto (chairman). *Report of the National Advisory Commission on Civil
    Disorders.* New York: Bantam, 1968.
Kittredge, Clare. "Group Returning to Radical Roots: Reunion Planned for
    Members of '60s 'Virtuous Caucus' Group." *Boston Globe*, July 18,
    1993.
Kornbluth, Jesse. *Notes from the New Underground.* New York: Viking, 1968.
———. "This Place of Entertainment Has No Fire Exit: The Underground
    Press and How It Went." *Antioch Review*, Spring 1969, 91–98.
———. *Head Butler: A Plugged-in Cultural Concierge.* www.headbutler.com/.
Lerner, Steve. "The Liberation of the Liberation News Service." *Village
    Voice*, August 22, 1968.
Lovejoy, Sam. "Somebody's Got to Do It." In Smith and Koster, *Time It
    Was*, 415–33.

Mareneck, Susan. "Ben Frank Moss, Painter." *Kansas Quarterly* 14.4 (Fall 1982): 43–54.

———. *Packaged Views.* New York: Lower East Side Printshop / See Through Books, 1990.

———. *Beyond a Unifying Light: The Work of Esme Thompson.* Exhibition catalogue. Hanover, NH: Dartmouth College, 1990.

———. "Double Dedication." *Spence School Centennial Bulletin,* 1992.

McLane, Daisanne. "MUSE: Rock Politics Comes of Age." *Rolling Stone,* November 15, 1979.

McMillian, John. *Smoking Typewriters: The Sixties Underground Press and the Rise of Alternative Media in America.* New York: Oxford University Press, 2011.

Mungo, Raymond. *Famous Long Ago: My Life and Hard Times with Liberation News Service.* Boston: Beacon Press, 1970; rev. ed., Amherst: University of Massachusetts Press, 2012.

———. *Total Loss Farm: A Year in the Life.* New York: E. P. Dutton, 1970.

———. *Beyond the Revolution: My Life and Times Since Famous Long Ago.* Chicago: Contemporary Books, 1990.

MUSE (Musicians United for Safe Energy). *The Muse Concerts for A Non-Nuclear Future.* (Concert performances, official program). New York, September 1979.

———. *No Nukes.* Recording. Producers: Jackson Browne, Graham Nash, John Hall, Bonnie Raitt. Elektra/Asylum Records, 1979.

———. *No Nukes.* Film. Producer: Julian Schlossberg. Directors: Danny Goldberg, Anthony Potenza. MUSE/Warner Brothers, 1980.

Nathan, Robert, and Howard Blum. "Some Other Memories of Marshall Bloom" (op-ed column). *New York Times,* May 19, 1973.

Payne, Harry. "Roll Over, Norman Rockwell: The Real 1950s." Talk delivered November 8, 1997. AC 9.1, Williams College. President. Addresses, 1994–1999.Williams College Archives & Special Collections, Williamstown, MA.

Plimpton, Oakes. *1975 Farm Journal: A Back-to-the-Land Movement Story.* Bloomington, IN: iUniverse, 2011.

Precht, Paul. "Fertile Fields for the Sixties: Montague Farm Looks Back 25 years." *Daily Hampshire Gazette* (Northampton, MA), August 14–15, 1993.

Queen, Christopher S. *Engaged Buddhism in the West.* Somerville, MA: Wisdom Publications, 2000.

Rodale, Robert. "Young People—Are They America's New Peasantry?" *Organic Gardening and Farming,* May, 1971, 30–33.

Rogers, Cathy. "Advice from the Naturopathic Midwife." In *Eat Right for Your Baby,* by Peter J. D'Adamo, ND. New York: G. P. Putnam's Sons, 2003.

———, associate ed. *Foundations of Naturopathic Medicine.* Amsterdam: Elsevier, forthcoming.

Simon, Peter. *Moving On/Holding Still.* New York: Grossman, 1972.

———. *I and Eye: Pictures of My Generation.* Boston: Little, Brown, 2001.

Slonecker, Blake. "Living the Movement: Liberation News Service, Montague Farm, and the New Left, 1967–81." PhD diss. University of North Carolina at Chapel Hill, 2009.

———. "We Are Marshall Bloom: Sexuality, Suicide, and the Collective Memory of the Sixties." *The Sixties: A Journal of History, Politics, and Culture* 3.2 (December 2010): 187–205.

———. *A New Dawn for the New Left: Liberation News Service, Montague Farm, and the Long Sixties.* New York: Palgrave Macmillan, 2013.

Smith, Karen Manners, and Tim Koster, eds. *Time It Was: American Stories from the Sixties.* Upper Saddle River, NJ: Pearson Prentice Hall, 2007.

Stevens, Amy. *Daniel Shays' Legacy? Marshall Bloom, Radical Insurgency and the Pioneer Valley.* Amherst, MA: Collective Copies, 2005.

Surbrug, Robert E., Jr. *Beyond Vietnam: The Politics of Protest in Massachusetts, 1974–1990.* Amherst: University of Massachusetts Press, 2009.

Vonnegut, Kurt. *Cat's Cradle.* New York: Dell, 1963.

Wasserman, Harvey. *Harvey Wasserman's History of the United States.* New York: Harper and Row, 1972.

———. *Energy War: Reports from the Front.* Westport, CT: Lawrence Hill, 1979.

———. *The Last Energy War: The Battle over Utility Deregulation.* New York: Seven Stories Press, 1999.

———, senior ed. *The Free Press* (online publication). www.freepress.org/.

Wasserman, Harvey, and Norman Solomon. *Killing Our Own: The Disaster of America's Experience with Atomic Radiation.* New York: Dell, 1982.

Williams, Paul. *Time Between*. New York: Entwhistle Books, 1972.

Wilton, John. *Raga Records: Live Concerts, Archival Recordings, North Indian Classical Music*. http://www.raga.com/

Wizansky, Richard, ed. *Home Comfort: Life on Total Loss Farm*. New York: Saturday Review Press, 1973.

ACKNOWLEDGMENTS

℘

Interviews

This book is based in part on my interviews, conversations, and correspondence with Michael Curry, Janice Frey, Sam Lovejoy, Susan Mareneck, Peter Natti, J. Carson Sloan, James Tapley, Harvey Wasserman, and numerous others in the farm's extended family. I have also drawn on interviews and other material compiled by Nora Jacobson, Tim Koster, Blake Slonecker, and Karen Manners Smith.

Research Sources

The Famous Long Ago Archive, an umbrella collection that focuses on the extended family of Montague Farm and includes subcollections focused on Steve Diamond, Ray Mungo, MUSE, and other aspects of the farm family, is located in the Special Collections and University Archives, University of Massachusetts Amherst Libraries (www.library.umass.edu /spcoll/). The archive's own websites are http://scua.wordpress.com and www.famouslongago.org/. The papers of Marshall Bloom are housed in Amherst College Archives and Special Collections. A number of other people and activities related to the extended farm family can be found through bibliographic research, as well as on the Web. Note that Beech River Books (www.beechriverbooks.com) is the publisher of a new edition of Steve Diamond's *What the Trees Said*, the early history of Montague Farm. A new edition of Ray Mungo's *Famous Long Ago* was published in 2012 by University of Massachusetts Press.

Farm members generously provided material on the farm's reunion in 1993. The voluminous farm family e-mails surrounding the farm's final disposition, from 2000 to 2002, offered a rich source for information on this period.

The Williams College Archives & Special Collections provided a copy of Harry Payne's "Roll Over, Norman Rockwell: The Real 1950s."

Readers, Advisors

Friends and colleagues who consulted on the story or the manuscript at some point include Daniel Aaron, Arlene Bouras, Simon Brennan, Rob Cox, Jennifer Fels, Sophie Fels, Jesse Kornbluth, Steve Lerner, John McMillian, Ray Mungo, Carl Oglesby, Blake Slonecker, and Bruce Wilcox.

Illustrations

For permission to use photographs and other reproductions I thank Laura Bradley, Laurie Cohen, Michael Curry, Lionel Delevingne, Emmanuel Dunand, Jennifer Fels, Ray Mungo, Eric Roth, Peter Simon, Jeremy Toal, Jack Vartoogian, John Wilton, and others with private collections, as well as the Famous Long Ago archive at the University of Massachusetts Amherst.

Tom Fels's four years on a communal farm, from 1969 to 1973, form the background for *Buying the Farm*. After 1981 he became a full-time curator and writer. Some of his many exhibitions have appeared at the J. Paul Getty Museum in Los Angeles and the Van Gogh Museum in Amsterdam. In 1986 he was named a Chester Dale Fellow of the Metropolitan Museum of Art, and in 1998 a Fletcher Jones Foundation Fellow of the Huntington Library. Mr. Fels currently pursues independent research and writing in culture and the arts, including the founding of the Famous Long Ago archive at the University of Massachusetts Amherst, which focuses on the extended family of Montague Farm highlighted in *Buying the Farm*. His *Farm Friends* (2008), also on the extended farm family, was widely praised and received an Eric Hoffer award. He lives with his wife in North Bennington, Vermont.

Daniel Aaron, the Victor S. Thomas Professor of English and American Literature Emeritus at Harvard University, is the author of *Writers on the Left* and numerous other works on American history and culture, and was founding president of the Library of America. In 2010 he received the National Humanities Medal, awarded for outstanding achievement in history, literature, education, and cultural policy.